HOW TO *REALLY* LOVE YOUR TEENAGER

Distributed by:

Australia
Christian Press,
3 Harley Crescent,
Condell Park 2200,
Sydney,
Australia.

New Zealand
Gospel Publishing House Society Ltd.,
154 King Street,
PO Box 74,
Palmerston North,
New Zealand.

Singapore
Scripture Union Distributors,
413 Tagore Avenue,
Singapore 2678.

South Africa
Christian Art Wholesale,
20 Smuts Avenue,
Box 1599,
Vereeniging 1930,
South Africa.

How to *really* love your Teenager

DR. ROSS CAMPBELL, M.D.

Scripture Press

Amersham-on-the-Hill, Bucks HP6 6JQ, England

© 1981 by SP Publications, Inc.
First published in the USA 1981 by Victor Books a division
of Scripture Press Publications, Inc., Wheaton, Illinois, USA

First British edition 1987
Reprinted 1988

ISBN 0 946515 22 0

Scripture quotations are from the *King James Version* (KJV); *The Living
Bible* (TLB), © 1971, Tyndale House Publishers, Wheaton, IL 60189;
and *The Modern Language Bible: The Berkeley Version in Modern
English* (MLB), © 1945, 1959, 1969 by the Zondervan Publishing House.
Used by permission.

Cover photograph: ACE Photo Agency – London

Production and printing in Great Britain for
SCRIPTURE PRESS FOUNDATION (UK) LTD
Raans Road, Amersham-on-the-Hill, Bucks HP6 6JQ by
Nuprint Ltd, Harpenden, Herts AL5 4SE

Contents

Foreword 7

Preface 9

1 The Teenager 13

2 The Home 21

3 Unconditional Love 31

4 Focused Attention 39

5 Eye Contact and Physical Contact 53

6 Parental Self-Control 63

7 Teenage Anger 73

8 From Parent Control to Self-Control 89

9 Adolescent Depression 105

10 Helping Your Teenager Intellectually 117

11 Helping Your Teenager Spiritually 125

12 The Older Adolescent 141

Foreword

by Roy & Fiona Castle

This is a penetrating book, but seeing teenagers through adolescence in today's world is no light matter. This book certainly gets down to the real issues of being a parent.

Parents haven't been trained to be parents, and so bringing up teenagers tends to be something done rather haphazardly. Even 'successes' seem to happen accidentally. This book will guide parents in the right directions for today's lifestyles.

The author, Dr Campbell, writes sensitively yet clearly about teenage depression and about how teenagers can express their anger in appropriate ways. He draws us back to such basics as whether we as parents really give our children 'unconditional love' and the quality of the time and attention we give them. All of the author's writing is set within a Christian framework—not one that just gives pat answers but one that is determined to find a realistic way of developing a deepening relationship with children in the difficult teenage years.

What appealed to us especially was the author's honesty in sharing not only sound principles but also his honesty in relating how these have worked out in his own family life. He doesn't shirk problems but offers some ways out, at the same time giving us instances of both his failures and successes. The thrust of the book is not to condemn us where we have failed, but to point to

7

better ways. What comes through strongly is the joy as well as the responsibilities of being a parent.

Dr Campbell writes as a psychiatrist but his style avoids jargon and is down to earth. We would recommend that you read this book before your children are teenagers. It's a practical book which you will want to read and re-read as you go through the teenage years with your children.

ROY & FIONA CASTLE

Preface

Guiding a child through the teenage years is a complex venture and one with which most parents today are having great difficulty. In almost every respect, the adolescent situation is becoming worse year after year. Teenage suicide has increased so dramatically that it is now the second leading cause of death for people between the ages of 14 and 20. Academic achievement scores and standards have steadily gone down over the last several years. Drug abuse, juvenile crime, teenage pregnancy, venereal disease, and feelings of despair are all statistically overwhelming.

What's wrong? The primary source of the problem usually lies with parents who do not have a balanced perspective about how to relate to their teenagers. Most parents have distorted ideas of what adolescence is and what they should expect of their young people.

Although most parents truly love their teenagers, they don't know how to convey that love in ways that make the teenagers feel loved and accepted. However, parents who really desire to give their teenagers what they need can learn to do so.

I have found that parents who put into practice the principles discussed in this book have a high degree of success in helping their teenagers develop properly and become responsible, mature, and conscientious adults.

Some of the foundation material for this book is from *How to Really Love Your Child.* Since the needs of teenagers are more complex than those of younger children, it is necessary to apply the information differently.

As you integrate the ideas in this book into a solid and balanced approach for relating to your teenager, I think you will be pleasantly surprised to discover how exciting and fulfilling it can be to really love your teenager.

9

1

The Teenager

Why did she do it—
didn't we do a good enough job as parents?

Teenagers are children in transition. They are not young adults. Their needs, including their emotional needs, are those of children. One of the most common mistakes parents, teachers, and others make regarding adolescents is to consider them junior adults. Many people in authority over teenagers overlook their childlike needs for feeling love and acceptance, for being taken care of, and for knowing that someone really cares for them.

Far too many teenagers today feel that no one really cares about them. As a result, many of them have feelings of worthlessness, hopelessness, helplessness, poor self-esteem, and self-depreciation.

Today's teenagers are described by many as the "apathetic generation." Why is this? Because so many teens see themselves in a negative way, as unappreciated and worthless. Such a self-concept is the natural result of a child not feeling genuinely loved and cared for.

Two of the most frightening results of this apathy are depression and revolt against authority. Apathetic teens can become easy prey for unscrupulous persons who use young people for their own ends. They are susceptible to being influenced by authoritarian groups that provide easy answers and impossible promises. But there are ways to prevent apathy in our teenagers, and to promote healthy, energetic, productive, and creative attitudes.

Parents and Teenagers

Parenting teenagers in today's world is difficult. One important reason for this is that most of a teenager's time is spent under the control and influence of others—schoolteachers, peers, neighbors, and television entertainers. Many people feel that regardless of how well they do their job as parents, their efforts have a small effect on their teenagers. But the opposite is true. For evidence indicates that the home wins hands down in every case. The home is stronger than any other influence in determining how happy, secure, and stable a teenager is; how he relates to adults, peers, or children; how confident he is in himself; and how he responds to new or strange situations. Regardless of the many distractions in the life of a teenager, the home has the deepest influence on his life.

I am so thankful that the home maintains the principal influence upon our children. For I want my children to be reflectors of our home. However, this places great responsibility upon my wife and me as parents.

A teenager may be bigger, smarter, stronger, or in other ways superior to his parents. But emotionally he is still a child. He continues to need to feel loved and accepted by his parents. Unless the teenager feels that priceless assurance of love and acceptance by his parents, he will not be his best or do his best. He cannot reach his potential.

Very few teenagers are fortunate enough to feel truly loved and accepted as they should be. It is true that most parents have deep feelings of love toward their teenagers. They assume, however, that they naturally and effectively convey this love. This is indeed the greatest error parents make today. For most parents are simply not transmitting or conveying their own heartfelt love to their teenagers. The reason is that they do not know how.

As we work with teenagers who have problems, a common,

interweaving thread constantly presents itself as either the cause or the aggravator of their troubled situations—a feeling of not being loved and cared for by their parents.

That is what this book is all about. It is a how-to book, to help parents know *how to* love their teenagers so they will be their best, act their best, and grow to become their best. I pray that it will be not only a book of answers for the weary, confused parent, but also a book of hope.

I, for one, love teenagers. They are about the dearest people I know. Given what they need emotionally, they are able to respond in such wholesome and joyful ways that sometimes I think my heart will burst.

Yes, they are definitely capable of trying us to our utter limits of tolerance and patience. Yes, sometimes we lose our cool and our tempers, and feel we simply do not have what it takes to meet their needs. We may even want to run away or give up.

But, dear parent, hang in there! Our perseverance is indeed worth it. For it is a priceless wonder to see our teenagers develop into pleasant and productive adults. But we must be realistic. This doesn't just happen. We must pay a price.

I truly want this book to be a source of hope to you. The last thing I want is to cause you to feel guilty. We all make mistakes. Just as there are no perfect children, there are no perfect parents. Don't let guilt from past mistakes damage your efforts to raise your teenagers well.

Most adolescent problems can be alleviated or rectified by correcting tensions in the parent-teenager relationship. However, there are some teenage problems which are caused or aggravated by neurological ills or physiological depression. These medical problems must be alleviated before attempting to correct parent-teenager relationships.

Debbie

"I can't believe she did it," explained Mrs. Batten, as she and Mr. Batten began unfolding their painful story in my counseling room.

"She was such a good girl, always content, never gave us much trouble. I thought we were giving Debbie everything she needed—clothes, church, good home, and all. She's always seemed happy.

"Why would she ever want to try to kill herself. How could she have taken all those pills? Does she really want to die, or is she just trying to get attention? I'm so confused. And she's gotten so hateful and sullen. I can't talk to her, and she won't talk to me. She just wants to spend time by herself in her room. And her grades have become terrible."

Mrs. Batten sat in her chair, her shoulders slumped, the sparkle missing from her usually bright eyes. As she told me more of her daughter's problems, I knew that she was as confused and lonely as Debbie. This was a very typical example of the gap in understanding how to love a teenager.

"When did you notice these changes in Debbie?" I asked.

"About two or three years ago," replied Mrs. Batten. "But it was so gradual we didn't think anything was seriously wrong until fairly recently. Let's see. She's 15 now. During the last few months of sixth grade we noticed she became bored—first with school. Her grades began falling. The teacher complained of her daydreaming and nonparticipation in class. She was very concerned about Debbie then. I wish we had listened to Mrs. Collins. She was such a fine teacher.

"Then Debbie gradually became bored with life. She gave up her favorite activities one by one and seemed to lose interest in everything, including church. She began to avoid her good friends and spend more and more time by herself. She talked less and less.

"But everything became even worse when she began seventh grade. She completely withdrew from her old standby friends and began running around with kids who were in trouble most of the time. Debbie's attitude worsened as she became more like her new friends. And they often led her into trouble—deep trouble.

"But we've tried almost everything," Mrs. Batten continued.

"First, we spanked her. Then we began taking away her privileges and freedoms. We've grounded her. We've tried rewarding her for good behavior. We've talked to everyone we thought might be able to help us. I really believe we have tried everything. Can Debbie really be helped?"

"We're desperate," Mr. Batten interjected. "Did we do a poor job as parents? We've certainly *tried* hard enough. Is it inherited? Maybe physical? Should we get a sugar test or an EEG? Will vitamins or minerals help? We love Debbie, Dr. Campbell. What can be done? Is it hopeless?"

I saw Debbie later after her parents left. She was a pretty girl with likeable ways. Although unquestionably intelligent, she had difficulty speaking in a clear, audible way. She communicated mostly in grunts with many "uh-huhs." Debbie did not have the natural spontaneity and enthusiasm we like to see in an early adolescent. She was obviously unhappy, and it was difficult to communicate with her.

However, when Debbie felt more comfortable, she spoke more freely, and her eye contact improved. She stated by her behavior and in her words that she had lost interest in all she once cared for. She finally said, "Nothing really matters. No one cares about me and I don't care about anything. It doesn't matter anyway."

As the conversation continued it became clear that Debbie was suffering from an increasingly frequent and serious adolescent problem—depression. She seldom had times when she felt content with herself or her life. For years Debbie had longed for a close, warm relationship with her parents, but during the past few months, she had gradually given up hope in this dream. More and more she turned to her peers, who she thought would accept her more lovingly; but her unhappiness deepened even more.

Debbie represents a common and tragic occurrence among early adolescent girls. Debbie *seemed* to be happy and content during her earlier years. During those years, she was a complacent child who made few demands on her parents, teachers, or others. So no one suspected that she did not feel genuinely loved and accepted by her parents. Even though she had parents who deeply loved her and cared for her, Debbie did not *feel* genuinely loved. Yes, Debbie intellectually knew of her parents' love and care for her, and never would have told you that they did not love her. But Debbie did not have the precious and crucial feeling of being completely and unconditionally loved and accepted.

This situation is difficult to understand because Debbie's parents are indeed fine parents. They love their daughter and look after her needs to the best of their ability and knowledge. Mr. and Mrs. Batten have attempted to carry out all that they have learned, and have also followed good advice from experts. In addition, their marriage is indeed a good one. They have a stable relationship and do love each other. Each treats the other with respect.

Yet, the Battens, like many parents today, are experiencing real difficulty in raising their children, and in understanding how to effectively guide them through the stages of their lives to young adulthood. With pressures increasing every day upon the American family, it is easy to become disheartened, confused, and pessimistic. Rising rates of divorce, economic and financial crises, decreasing quality of education, and declining trust in leadership—all place emotional hardships on everyone. As we parents suffer increasing physical, emotional, and spiritual strain, it becomes more and more difficult to care for our teenagers. I believe that a child, especially a teenager, pays the greatest price during these difficult times. A teenager is the most vulnerable person in our society, and his deepest need is love.

Debbie's parents have carried out their parental responsibility in raising their daughter to the best of their ability—but something is not right. Debbie does not *feel* genuinely loved. Is it the parents' fault? Are they to be blamed? I do not believe they should be. Mr. and Mrs. Batten have always loved Debbie but have never known how to convey their love. As with most parents, they have a vague notion of the needs of a child—protection, shelter, food, clothes, education, guidance, love, etc. They have met essentially all these needs except unconditional love.

I believe parents who really desire to give their teenagers what they need can be taught to do so. Parents need to learn how to genuinely and effectually *transmit* their love to their teenagers. And that is what this book is about.

2

The Home

*The most important relationship in the home
is the marriage bond.*

The first responsibility of parents is to provide a loving and happy home. And the most important relationship in the home is the marriage bond, which takes primacy over the parent-child relationship. The security of the teenager and the quality of the parent-child bonding are largely dependent on the quality of the marital bonding. You can see how important it is to assure the best possible relationship between husband and wife, since this is the basis for seriously attempting to relate to the teenager in a more positive way.

Chuck

Chuck's parents brought him to me because of truancy, stealing, and disobedience. The Hargraves talked about their son with frustration and anger. The intensity of their negative feelings toward the boy concerned me.

Chuck said nothing but sat solemnly with his eyes downcast while he listened to his parents' accusations. When he finally spoke, he did so in a soft, meek voice and with short phrases rather than sentences.

I spent some time with Chuck alone after his parents left the office. He was angry, but he couldn't tell me exactly why. It soon became evident that Chuck was a confused boy. He was confused about himself and about the relationship between his parents. He was also puzzled regarding his misconduct, for he was a bright boy who had not experienced academic problems. He was well liked by his peers, and had no unusual problems with his teachers. He was also confused about his stealing, since he did not need the items that he took. And it was obvious that he had set himself up to be caught.

Chuck's case is not unusual. Although his parents mean well, they have made several mistakes in raising Chuck. Their marriage is in trouble, largely because they have not learned to share their feelings and opinions with each other. Mrs. Hargrave has never been able to express her normal anger in an open, healthy, direct way to her husband; therefore she manifests her anger by getting back at him in subtle and indirect ways—such as overspending. Mr. Hargrave, who feels unable to be openly honest with his wife, expresses his anger by being silent, avoiding eye contact, and evading family and home responsibilities.

Chuck has learned his lesson well. Because open, honest discussion and expression of feelings do not exist in the Hargrave home, Chuck demonstrates his anger by doing things which embarrass and upset his parents.

Due to lack of normal communication, Mr. and Mrs. Hargrave have never understood each other's feelings and expectations regarding Chuck. So they have never agreed on behavioral limits or appropriate discipline for Chuck.

This has been confusing to Chuck, for he has never known his parents' expectations of him. He was a boy who naturally wanted to please. But how could he? He gave up trying to live up to his parents' standards, because he never knew what they were.

All these problems existed because the parents were never able to talk things out between them and come to mutual decisions.

Roger

Let me share another illustration that shows the importance of the marital relationship in raising a teenager. Roger is a 14-year-old boy who was caught breaking into a home and stealing several items. His parents brought him to me because he was failing in school, had developed a defiant attitude, and was usually in a sullen mood. A history revealed that Roger's parents had been having problems with him for several years. He usually disobeyed, constantly challenged parental authority, and would get his way by manipulation. He used what one parent said against the other. These tactics caused conflict between the parents. Mom and Dad fought about how to handle Roger, while Roger did as he pleased.

Evaluation revealed that Roger had perceptual problems, was deeply depressed, and exhibited passive-aggressive traits (to be discussed in chapter 7). When I gave them my recommendations, Roger's parents, in their typical way of handling problems, argued with each other about what should be done. Even with professional recommendations, these unfortunate parents were unable to come to logical and sensible decisions regarding their son.

Of course, one of my main objectives in this case was to help the parents improve their own relationship, so that they would be united regarding the discipline of Roger. For only then would the boy respect his parents, stop using one against the other, and learn to control himself in appropriate ways.

Need for Communication

These illustrations reveal how problems in marital relationships can produce difficulties among our teenagers. Every teenager needs parents whose marital relationship is one of stability, respect, love, and good communication.

The ability to communicate feelings, especially unpleasant feelings, is critical in the marital relationship. Especially during times of stress, this honest, open talking it out is absolutely critical and can determine whether stress will enhance or break a marriage.

In my own marriage I have discovered this importance of communications over and over, and usually the hard way. I believe the most stressful period of our marriage was right after the birth of our second daughter, Cathy, who was born with several physical deformities. I had a difficult enough time handling this. But when she was about a year old, it slowly became apparent that Cathy was profoundly mentally retarded along with having cerebral palsy, and a severe seizure disorder. As a 24-year-old husband and father, I experienced feelings that I did not know were possible. I felt anger, rage, extreme pain, and feelings of guilt and inadequacy as a man, father, and husband. I could hardly bear it. Many times I just wanted to run, especially as we saw no improvement in Cathy's condition. She was developing no self-help skills or physical abilities.

Cathy was a child-care nightmare. When she could finally move herself along the floor, she would head straight to the garbage can and try to eat the garbage (or anything else she could put in her mouth). She had little sense of pain and would often attempt to place her hands on the hot stove burners. Cathy had to be watched closely every second because her constant striving was toward doing things which were dangerous to her.

All this began in my first year of medical school. With Cathy's expenses and the pressures of medical school, our financial situation was quite bleak. I remember wondering many times how our marriage could possibly survive.

Pat has always been the more emotionally mature partner in our marriage. The pain about Cathy and our untenable situation was just as difficult for her as it was for me. But her response was so different from mine. In the midst of constant heartbreak, Pat carefully looked after Cathy's every need with patience, gentleness, and devoted love. She seldom gave in to the agonizing feelings which were driving me away. Her inner beauty of love, gentleness, and patience were beyond my comprehension. And, worst of all, I couldn't appreciate her qualities as I should have, because they contrasted with my inability to cope with the situation. I felt her maturity made me look rather bad as a husband and father. I somewhat resented her for this and tended to pull away from her and Cathy whenever I reasonably could.

Yet I truly loved Pat, and I realized that instead of helping her, I was adding to her crushing burden. So I felt guilty and utterly helpless. I went to several people seeking help on how to deal with this agony. But no one knew what I was talking about.

I believe things came to their absolute worst when the "patterning" method of treating children like Cathy came into vogue. It took five people to move her arms, legs, and head in coordinated movements to simulate the movements of crawling. This required our family's total resources for several hours each day. The utterly crushing consumption of time and effort came close to being the ton that broke the Campbells' back.

Eventually we found, as did many others, that there is flimsy rationale for patterning. It turned out to be a total waste of time. But before this conclusion was finally drawn, our family was in shambles.

Yet even at this point of profound gloom, Pat continued her motherly care with gentleness, love, and unbelievable patience. She had not lost her inner peace and incredible inner beauty.

Me? I was hardly coping. I hurt inside for Cathy from morning to night. I had difficulty concentrating on my studies, and kept wondering how we were going to manage financially. In short, I was miserable and feared that we could not survive much longer. I wondered, "How much stress can a marital relationship be expected to bear? Will it break or simply die?"

By this time Cathy was five years old. The situation was generally the same, but her seizures were becoming worse and were less and less controlled by medication. Eventually the slightest environmental change would set off another seizure. Cathy would not eat for three days following a seizure. When the frequency increased to several a day, forced-tube feeding became necessary. It finally became obvious that Cathy could not survive outside of a hospital. Then came the most difficult, agonizing decision and day of our lives—we had to permanently place Cathy in a hospital for the mentally retarded. Imagine—turning our precious five-year-old daughter over to people we didn't even know. I wasn't sure I could handle this one at all. But, again, I noticed my dear, dear wife, Pat. Struggling with just as much pain and agony as I , she knew what we had to do, made the decision, found the courage to accept it, and never lost her inner peace and beauty.

I learn slowly. But this time, instead of fighting an unchangeable situation down to my last guilt-ridden ounce of energy (including resenting my wife's beautiful way of responding to life's most unbearable agonies), I decided that I had much to learn from her. She had taught me, as only a woman can do, how to live with life's most unbearable situations.

Every type of personality has its advantages and disadvantages. In the situation with Cathy, Pat was the stronger and I needed to learn from her, and sometimes lean on her. In other situations, I happen to be better able to cope, and then I can help Pat.

The point of all this is to understand that stress will come into every marriage. Whether the stress hurts and destroys the marriage, or enhances it, depends on the *response* of husband and wife. My initial response to a cruel situation was destructive. I tended to avoid it, leaving Pat to handle the entire burden by herself. By her consistent example, she showed me how to live out my commitments as husband and father and to take my responsibility. As I did, my appreciation and love for her mushroomed. Because I learned to cope with inner pain rather than to run from it, Pat and I are now able to face together those problems which produce emotional pain.

Fellow parents, if we persevere through the problems which put stress on our marriages, we will grow as spouses. If we continue to carry out our marital responsibility as a *lifelong commitment,* we will grow together in love, appreciation, and respect. We must live and think as though there are no other alternatives than to *make this marriage work.* Yes, it *is* work. It is *hard work.* And it takes this lifelong commitment of both spouses. Many marriages today are based on a "wait-and-see" attitude—"We'll give it a try and if it doesn't pan out, we'll split." No marriage can truly succeed on that basis. Is there anything more rare today than total, lifelong commitment to marriage? Our way of life has been based on the integrity of the family. Yet unless it is rekindled and enhanced, the institution of marriage may be doomed.

Role Reversal

A situation that is rather common today is the role reversal in which a parent demands that a child fulfill the parent's emotional needs. While this can happen in any home, it is more likely to occur in a one-parent family.

Some single parents feel tempted to use their teenagers as colleagues or confidants. This is more difficult for them to deal with because they do not have spouses with whom to share the adult levels of the home.

Because of loneliness, feelings of inadequacy, depression, or other causes, single parents at times find it difficult to avoid relating to their teenagers as contemporaries. These parents may share intimately personal information which the teenagers are not ready to handle. Such parents tend to be "best friends" with their teenagers, instead of maintaining healthy parent-child relationships.

I have seen extreme examples of this. Jim was a 16-year-old boy who frequently would get drunk with his father in a bar. Although this happened because of the father's loneliness and lack of friends, the father rationalized to himself that he was "making a man" of his son.

I remember Julie whose mother would have her boyfriend bring a date for Julie so they could go out together. While these are obviously extreme examples, role reversal is not unusual. Lesser forms of misusing teenagers in this way are very common. For example, parents complain to teenage children about how lonely, depressed, unhappy, or misused they are. This is *not* parenting. A parent fulfills the emotional needs of a child or a teenager. For the teenager to fill the emotional needs of a parent is "reversal of roles" and is unwholesome. A teenager treated in this way *cannot* develop normally.

Whether we are single or married, we parents must always maintain our position as mother or father in the home. We are responsible to meet the emotional needs of our teenagers. If we reverse this natural course and look to them to emotionally nourish us, we will hurt them—and destroy our relationship with them. We must obtain our emotional nourishment elsewhere—not from our children.

I have never particularly enjoyed being an authority for anyone, especially for my children. I too am tempted to treat my children as contemporary friends, but I dare not. Yes, I am loving and friendly with them and enjoy laughing and having fun. And on occasion, I will share appropriate personal information with them, but only for their educational benefit—*not for my emotional benefit*. I must not forget that I am their father and that they need my authority and direction. If I relinquish or neglect my responsibility for being the authority in the home—along with Pat, for she too must assume her position of authority—my children will not be happy. They will feel insecure, and will be very apt to develop poor behavior patterns.

I must not use my children or teenagers as counselors, shoulders to cry on, emotional support, or colleagues. Of course, I can ask their opinion or advice on occasion, as long as I am not doing it in ways that prompt them to nourish me emotionally. I cannot ask them to make me feel better. There is no way to be consistently firm with my teenagers if I am dependent on them for my emotional support.

As parents, our first responsibility is to make our children feel genuinely loved. Our second responsibility is to be authority figures for our children and to lovingly discipline them.

3

Unconditional Love

Saying *'I love you'* is not enough.

The basic foundation for a solid relationship with your teenager is unconditional love. For only unconditional love can prevent problems such as resentment, guilt, fear, or the insecurity of feeling unwanted.

Only if your basic relationship with your teenager is built on unconditional love can you be confident in your parenting. Without this foundation, it is impossible to really understand your teenager, or know how to guide him, or deal with his behavior.

Without unconditional love, parenting is a confusing and frustrating burden. This love acts as a guiding light, showing you where you are with your teenager and what to do next. When you begin with unconditional love, you can then build your knowledge and expertise in guiding your teenager and filling his needs on a daily basis. You will also know where you are succeeding as a parent and where you are not.

You want to feel good about yourself as a parent. Many people question if this is possible. Let me assure you that it is very possible both to *be* a good parent and to *feel* confident that you are.

What Is Unconditional Love?

Unconditional love means loving a teenager, no matter what.

- No matter what the teenager looks like.
- No matter what his assets, liabilities, and handicaps are.
- No matter how he acts.

This does not mean that you always like his bahavior. Unconditional love means you love your teenager, even when you detest his behavior.

Unconditional love is an ideal. You can't love a teenager—or anyone else—100 percent of the time. But the closer you come to this goal, the more satisfied and confident you will feel. And the more pleasant and satisfied your teenager will be.

I, for one, cannot feel love for my teenagers all the time. But I will give myself credit for trying to arrive at that wonderful goal of loving them unconditionally. I help myself by constantly keeping in mind that:

- Teenagers *are* children.
- Teenagers will tend to act like teenagers.
- Much of teenage behavior is unpleasant.
- If I do my part as a parent and love them despite their unpleasant behavior, they will be able to mature and give up their immature ways.
- If I love them only when they please me (conditional love), and convey my love to them only during those times, they will not feel genuinely loved. This in turn will make them feel insecure, damage their self-image, and actually prevent them from developing more mature behavior. Therefore, their behavior development is as much my responsibility as theirs.
- If I love them unconditionally, they will feel good about themselves and be comfortable with themselves. They will be able to control their anxiety and, in turn, their behavior, as they grow into adulthood.
- If I love them only when they meet my requirements or expectations, they will feel incompetent. They will believe it is

33

fruitless to do their best because it is never enough. Insecurity, anxiety, and low self-esteem will plague them. There will be constant hindrances in their emotional and behavioral growth. Again, their total growth is as much my responsibility as theirs.

● For my sake, as a struggling parent, and for the sake of my children, I pray my love for them will be as unconditional as I can make it. The future of my teenagers depends on this foundation.

"Do You Love Me?"

Do you know what is the most important question on your teenager's mind? Without realizing it, he is continually asking, "Do you love me?" It is absolutely the most important question in the teenager's life. And he asks the question primarily through his behavior, rather than with words.

"Do you love me?" The answer you give to that question is absolutely critical. If you answer it no, your teenager will not be or do his best. You need to answer it yes, but few parents do. It is not that these parents don't love their teenagers. The problem is that most parents do not know how to answer yes; they don't know how to convey their love to their teenagers.

If you love your teenager unconditionally, he feels the answer is yes. If you love him conditionally, he is unsure and prone to anxiety. Your answer to that critical question, "Do you love me?" pretty well determines your teenager's basic attitude toward life. How crucial!

One of the main reasons most parents do not know how to convey their love to their teenager is because teenagers, like younger children, are *behaviorally oriented.* Adults are primarily *verbally oriented.*

Let me give you an illustration. As I am sitting here in the North Carolina mountains writing, my family is in Chattanooga. If I had a telephone here, I could make my wife the happiest woman in Hamilton County. I would call her and say something like, "Hi, Pat. I just wanted to tell you how much I love you." She would be on cloud nine.

But if I took the same phone and called my nine-year-old Dale and said, "Hi, Dale. This is your daddy. I just wanted to tell you I love you"—you know what his reaction would probably be? "Yes, Daddy, but why did you call?"

See the difference? My wife is verbally oriented, and verbal expression of love is deeply meaningful to her. My son is behaviorally oriented. While my verbal expression of love to him is important, it is simply insufficient to make him really feel loved, genuinely and unconditionally. If I called my 13-year-old son David, his reaction would be almost exactly like Dale's. My verbal expression of love would be much more meaningful to my 20-year-old daughter, Carey, but still not as much as to Pat.

Having a warm feeling of love in your heart for your teenager is wonderful—but it's not enough! Saying "I love you" to a teenager is great, and should be done—but it's not enough. For your teenager to *know* and *feel* you love him, you must also love him behaviorally because he is still primarily behaviorally oriented. Only then can he answer yes to the crucial question in his heart: "Do you love me?" Your teenager sees your love for him by what you *say* and *do*. But what you *do* carries more weight. Your teenager is far more affected by your actions than by your words.

It is also important to remember that your teenager has an emotional tank. This tank is figurative, of course, but the concept is very real. Your teenager has certain emotional needs, and whether these emotional needs are met (through love, understanding, discipline, etc.) helps determine how he feels—whether he is content, angry, depressed, or joyful. Also, it strongly affects his behavior—whether he is obedient, disobedient, whiny, perky, playful, or withdrawn. Naturally, the fuller the tank, the more positive the feelings and the better the behavior.

At this point let me make one of the most important statements in this book. ONLY IF THE EMOTIONAL TANK IS FULL, CAN A TEENAGER BE EXPECTED TO BE HIS BEST AND DO HIS BEST. It is your responsibility as a parent to do all you can to keep the emotional tank full.

Love Reflectors

Children and teenagers may be conceptualized as mirrors. They generally reflect rather than initiate love. If love is given to them, they return it. If none is given, they have none to return. Unconditional love is reflected unconditionally, and conditional love is returned conditionally.

As an example of mirrored love, let's think again about Debbie, whom we met in chapter 1. The love between Debbie and her parents was an example of a conditional relationship. Unfortunately, her parents felt that they should continually prompt her to do better by withholding praise, warmth, and affection, except for truly outstanding behavior (when she made them feel proud). Otherwise, they withheld love, feeling that too much approval and affection would spoil her and lessen her striving to be better. As Debbie grew older, she increasingly felt that her parents really didn't love or appreciate her in her own right, that they cared only about their own esteem as parents.

By the time Debbie was a teenager, she had learned well from her parents how to love conditionally. She behaved in a way which pleased her parents only when her parents did something special for her. Of course, with both Debbie and her parents now behaving this way, neither could convey love to the other because each was waiting for the other to do something first.

This is a typical result of conditional love. Love-giving eventually stops until another person does something very pleasing to get it going again. Everyone becomes more and more disappointed, confused, and bewildered. Eventually depression, anger, and resentment set in. In the Battens' case, this prompted them to seek help.

Emotional Tanks

As we mentioned before, teenagers are *children* emotionally. To illustrate this, let's look at how a teenager is like a two-year-old. Both a teenager and a two-year-old have drives for independence and both have emotional tanks. Each will strive for independence, using the energy from the emotional tank. When the emotional tank has run dry, the teenager and the two-year-old will do the same thing—return to the parent for a refill so they can again strive for independence.

For example, suppose a mother brings her two-year-old to a new place, such as a PTA meeting. At first the child may cling to his mother for emotional support. With a full emotional tank, the child will then begin exerting his independence by exploring. At first he may simply stand next to his mother and look around. As his emotional tank becomes empty, the child will seek his mother again for a refill with eye contact, physical contact, and focused attention. Now the child is again ready to try his independence. This time he may get to the end of the row before running out of emotional gasoline. Or he may interact with another person sitting close-by before his emotional tank runs dry.

Do you see the pattern? The child must repeatedly return to the parent to have his emotional tank refilled in order to continue his quest for independence. This is exactly what happens with the teenager, especially the early adolescent. He may use different means of exerting his drive for independence (and sometimes in disturbing or upsetting ways). He needs the energy from his emotional tank to do this. And where does he get his emotional tank refilled? Right! From his parents. A teenager will strive for independence in typical adolescent ways—doing things by himself, going places without family, testing parental rules. But he will eventually run out of emotional gasoline and come back to the parent for emotional maintenance—for a refill. This is what we want, as parents of teenagers. We want our adolescent *to be able* to come to us for emotional maintenance when he needs it.

There are several reasons why this refilling is so important.

● Teenagers need an ample amount of emotional nurturance if they are to function at their best and grow to be their best.

● They desperately need full emotional tanks in order to feel the security and self-confidence they must have to cope with peer pressure and other demands of adolescent society. Without this confidence, teenagers tend to succumb to peer pressure and experience difficulty in upholding wholesome, ethical values.

● The emotional refilling is crucial, because while it is taking place, it is possible to keep open lines of communication between parents and teenagers. When a teenager's tank is empty and he seeks parental love, communication is so much easier.

Most parents do not realize how important it is for their teenager to be able to come to them to have his emotional tank refilled. During times when a teenager is striving for independence, he may upset his parent to such an extent that the parent overreacts emotionally, and usually with excessive anger. This emotional overreaction, if too excessive or frequent, makes it extremely difficult, and perhaps impossible, for the teenager to return to his parents for emotional refills. Then, if parent-child communication is broken, a teenager may turn to his peers for emotional nurturance. What a dangerous, and frequently disastrous, situation this is! For the teenager will then be easily susceptible to peer pressure, to influences of religious cults, and to unscrupulous persons who use young people.

When your teenager tests you by striving through inappropriate behavior to be independent, you must be careful not to overreact emotionally. This does not mean condoning the misbehavior. You need to express your feelings honestly but appropriately; that is, without extreme anger, yelling, name-calling, attacking the child verbally, or otherwise losing control of yourself. Look at it this way. If someone you know overreacts with a temper tantrum, how are your feelings toward him affected? Your respect for that person lessens, especially if he loses self-control often.

The more a parent loses self-control in a teenager's presence, the less respect a teenager will feel for his parent. You should make every effort to maintain emotional control of yourself, regardless of how your teenager expresses his drive for independence. You must keep open the avenues over which your teenager returns to you to have his emotional tank refilled. This is crucial if he is to enter adulthood as a whole person.

4

Focused Attention

**Make your teenager feel
the most important person in the world to you.**

Giving focused attention to your teenager requires time. This is why it is more difficult to give than eye or physical contact. Eye contact and physical contact seldom require real sacrifice by parents. Focused attention does. It requires time and sometimes a lot of it. It may mean giving your teenager focused attention when you would rather do something else. For there are times when a teenager desperately needs focused attention that parents least feel like giving it.

Focused attention means giving your teenager full, undivided attention in such a way that he feels truly loved, that he knows he is so valuable in his own right that he warrants your watchfulness, appreciation, and uncompromising regard. Focused attention makes your teenager feel that he is the most important person in the world to you, his parents.

In the Scriptures, we see a very high regard for children. King David called them the heritage of the Lord. Christ said that no one should prevent the little ones from coming to Him, and warned that those who offend His little ones would be better dead. He said that unless we become as children before Him, we will not enter the kingdom of God. (See Psalm 127:3-5; Matthew 18:1-10; Mark 10:13-16.)

Teenagers ought to be made to feel that they are special. Few teenagers feel this way, but, oh, the difference it makes in them when they know they are special. Only focused attention can tell them this. It is so vital to the development of their self-esteem. And it profoundly affects their ability to relate to and love others.

I believe that focused attention is the most demanding need a teenager has. Most parents have real difficulty recognizing this need, much less fulfilling it. There are many reasons for this. For example, other things they do for their teenagers—favors, gifts, and granting unusual requests—seem to substitute for focused attention at the time. These things may be good, but it is a serious mistake to use them to replace genuine focused attention. This substitution is tempting to parents, because favors and gifts are easier to give, and take much less time. But teenagers do not do their best, do not feel their best, and do not behave their best unless they receive that precious commodity—focused attention from their parents.

Priorities

It is not possible for me to take care of every obligation and responsibility in my life in the way I would like to. There just isn't the time. So what can I do about this? There is only one answer, and it isn't simple—I must determine my priorities, set my goals, and plan my time to accomplish them. I must control my time in order to take care of the important things first.

What are the priorities in your life? Where do your children fit into them? Do they take first priority? Second? Third? You must determine this. Otherwise, your children will take a low precedence and suffer from some degree of neglect. No one else can decide for you what is important in your life.

Because life is so unpredictable, you cannot count on unlimited opportunities for nurturing your children. Therefore, you must take advantage of opportunities which you plan or which present themselves through your teenager's need. These will be fewer than you think you will have. Your children are teenagers for such a short time.

Necessity of Focused Attention

Focused attention is not something that is simply nice to give your teenager if time permits. It is a critical need each teenager has. How he views himself and how he is accepted by his world is determined primarily by the way in which this need is met. Without focused attention a teenager experiences increased anxiety, because he feels everything else is more important than he is. He is consequently less secure and becomes impaired in his emotional and psychological growth.

Such a teenager can be identified rather easily. He is generally less mature or sure of himself than teens whose parents have taken the time to fill their need for focused attention. This unfortunate teenager is often withdrawn and has difficulty with peers. He is less able to cope and usually reacts poorly in conflict. He is overly dependent on others, including peers, and is more subject to peer pressure.

Some young teenagers, however, especially girls deprived of focused attention from their fathers, seem to react in just the opposite way. They are quite talkative, manipulative, dramatic, and often seductive. They are sometimes considered precocious, outgoing, and mature as children. But as they grow older, this behavior pattern does not mature, and gradually becomes more inappropriate. By the time they are older teenagers, they are usually obnoxious to their peers as well as to adults. However, even at this late date, focused attention, especially from their fathers, can go a long way in reducing their self-defeating behavior, decreasing their anxiety, and freeing them to resume their maturational growth.

How Do You Give Focused Attention?

I have found that the best way to give a teenager focused attention is to set aside time to spend with him alone. You may already be thinking how difficult that is to do. And you are right. Finding time to be alone with a teenager, free from other distractions, is what I consider to be the most difficult aspect of good child-rearing. But let's face it—good child-rearing takes time. Finding time in our hyperactive society is hard, especially when teenagers have other interests with which the parents must compete. But this points all the more to the fact that focused attention is crucial. Today teenagers are more influenced by forces outside the family than ever before in history.

It takes tremendous effort to pry time from busy schedules; but when you do, the rewards are great. For it is a wonderful thing to see your teenager happy, secure, well-liked by peers and adults, and learning and behaving at his best. But such satisfaction does not come automatically. As parents you must pay a price for it. You must find time to spend alone with each child.

Time is difficult to manage. I try to conserve as much time as possible for my children. For example, when my daughter was taking music lessons near my office on Monday afternoons, I would schedule my appointments so that I could pick her up. Then we would stop at a restaurant and have supper together. At these times, without the pressure of interruption and time schedules, I was able to give her my full attention and listen to whatever she wanted to talk about.

Only in this context of being alone without pressure can parents and their child develop that special, indelible relationship which each child so desperately needs, to face the realities of life. A child treasures moments such as these, and remembers them when life becomes difficult, especially during those tumultuous years of adolescent conflict.

During times of focused attention, parents can make special opportunities for eye contact and physical contact with a child or teenager. For during these times of focused attention, eye and physical contact have stronger meaning and impact upon a child's life.

It is important that you watch for unexpected opportunities to spend additional time with your teenager. For example, you may find yourself alone with your teenager in moments when everyone else has gone away or is outside. You can take this as another opportunity to fill his emotional tank and to prevent problems brought on by a dry one. This time of focused attention may be quite short—but just a moment or two can do wonders.

Every moment counts, for the stakes are high. What is worse than a wayward, adolescent son or daughter? What is more wonderful than a well-balanced teenager?

Focused attention is time-consuming, difficult to do consistently, and many times burdensome for already exhausted parents. But focused attention is the most powerful means of keeping a teenager's emotional tank full and investing in his future.

As children grow older, these times of focus need to be lengthened. Older children need time to warm up, to let their developing defenses down, and to feel free to share their innermost thoughts, especially those that may be troubling them.

As children enter adolescence, they need *more* time with family, not less. It is so easy to assume that since teens are rapidly becoming more independent and *seem* to want more and more time away from the family, that you should spend less and less time with them. This is one of the most devastating mistakes parents make today. As their children enter and progress through adolescence, parents often use their free time in ways which meet their *own* pleasure needs. Every teenager I've ever known interprets this as rejection, feeling that their parents care less and less about them.

Adolescents need parental time and attention as never before. They are facing strong influences daily and, unfortunately, many of these influences are unhealthy, unwholesome, and sometimes evil. If you want your teenager to be able to cope with today's world, you must spend constructive time with him; especially when he is going through adolescent turmoils. If you do take the time to meet these needs, your teenager will gain the confidence and personal integrity to think for himself about the kind of values he will live by. He will develop strength to stand up against divisive influences from people who have little or no regard for him, but simply want to use him.

This may seem difficult to accomplish, especially when your

child is in a difficult, noncommunicative mood so commonly seen in early to middle adolescents. One secret to remember is that the psychological defenses of a moody teenager are very high, and that *time* is required for them to slowly be lowered to where the teenager is able to genuinely communicate and share with you what is *really* on his mind. Did you catch that magic word? TIME.

I remember when my precious daughter, Carey, was 14 years old. What a year! She was undergoing the typical transitions of early adolescence and would frequently communicate only with grunts like "uh-huh," "huh-uh," or "huh?"

During this period, I made two wonderful discoveries. First, it is useless *and* harmful to try to force a child to open up and talk at such a time. Although it was a real temptation to badger her with questions, I discovered this was a mistake and actually worsened the situation. Second, if I spent at least 20 to 30 minutes with Carey in a pleasant way which did not put any pressure on her to communicate, her defenses would slowly come down and we were then able to really share thoughts and feelings.

One of the most effective ways to accomplish that was to take her to a restaurant. I would pick the restaurant with the slowest service in town, and would try to arrive during the busiest time so we could wait in a long line. I would ask the waitress to come back a couple of times—"We're not quite ready to order." I would eat very slowly and then order a dessert, which I normally avoid, followed by a leisurely cup of coffee.

You see, the purpose of all this was to provide a time together when Carey was under no pressure to communicate and could still be comfortable in my presence. Standing in line in a public place meets this requirement. Other examples include fishing, hunting, hiking, taking a trip (short or long), playing a game, seeing a play, listening to an orchestra. When the teenager is with the parent but under no pressure, "just being there," the defenses will *gradually* come down, and the teenager will begin to talk—superficially at first, and then at more meaningful levels.

By the time we finished eating, Carey would be talking fairly freely and sharing—but with the conversation still at a rather superficial level—sports, teachers, schoolwork. Then I would pay the bill and we would go to the car.

Let me interject an interesting piece of information here. When you are driving a car with your teenager as a passenger, especially if other teenagers are with you, you somehow lose your own identity and are considered as part of the car—an extension of the steering wheel. My wife and I have really appreciated this adolescent ability—it is amazing how this facilitates adolescent conversation while riding along in the car. It is likewise amazing how much we have learned during these times.

Anyway, back to Carey and me. We would get in the car and usually, during the last mile or so before getting home, she would finally talk about things which were very meaningful to her. Things like peer relationships, family relationships, peer pressure to take drugs. Of course, the conversation couldn't be completed before we drove up to the house, typical of teenagers. The reason for this is that teenagers need to feel they have a means of "escape" when revealing meaningful information. They must feel that they are in a position to leave, if the parents are not responding properly to their innermost feelings. What they fear most is not disagreement but anger, ridicule, disapproval, or rejection of them on a personal level. They must feel enough in control so that if they become too uncomfortable, they can remove themselves.

This is why Carey would wait until we were near home before she would share with me what was really important to her. So the best conversations I had with Carey were at these times. Sometimes she would disguise her own conflicts by talking about or asking about another teenager who happened to have similar problems. This is a favorite way many teenagers use to talk about awkward, embarrassing, difficult-to-handle situations.

Sometimes a teenager needs to talk to a parent about a problem but has a difficult time initiating the conversation. At such times, he will frequently throw out hints. These hints can take various forms. A teenager who needs to talk, but who is in a noncommunicative mood, may say something much less threatening than what he actually wants to talk about. For example, he may start out by asking a question about homework. Perhaps a question about the day which the parent has had. Or maybe a comment about the day he has had.

Parents must be alert for such unsolicited and sometimes puzzling gestures. They are usually a hesitant teenager's way of asking for time and for focused attention. He is "feeling us out," testing us to see what kind of mood and frame of mind we are in—to see if it is safe to approach us on an issue about which he feels uncomfortable.

At other times, a teenager may test our receptivity, to see if we are in a good mood, by putting out what I call a "red herring," or "smoke screen." These are pieces of information designed to upset or irritate us—a perfect device to see if we can be trusted with what is *really* on his mind. If we overreact, especially with anger and criticism, the teenager assumes we will react to his important question the same way. Again, the more self-control and calmness we display, the more open and sharing our teenager will be with us.

These moments of opportunity are priceless. If we do not notice them and somehow close the door to the teenager, he will feel rejected. If we are alert and can detect these subtle clues, we can respond appropriately and help our teenagers, as well as demonstrate conclusively that we love him and are sensitive to his needs.

I remember many such occasions when Carey was in her early teens. Most often she would select a time when she knew her mother and I were alone with the least likelihood of interruption. You can guess when this was—just as Pat and I were ready to turn off the light for a good night's sleep. Carey's younger brothers were fast asleep, so she had no competition. First, we would see the door slowly open as Carey came in and asked her mother if she could borrow something from the adjoining bathroom. After Carey got the item she asked for and was in the process of leaving, she would turn around, and say to us, "Oh, by the way."

I can't overemphasize the importance of recognizing and noting these all too familiar words—"Oh, by the way," or their equivalent. Do you know what they usually really mean, when said by a teenager in such a situation? A translation is sometimes like this, "The real reason I'm here, and what I really want to talk about, is coming up. But first I want to know—are you in a good frame of mind to handle it? Can I trust you with this very delicate personal part of my life. Will you take it and help me, or will you use it against me? Can I trust you?"

If we do not give that focused attention at such a time, a teen will interpret the answer to be no. But if we focus our attention directly on the child, and listen intently and quietly, letting him control the conversation, our teenager will feel it is safe to take a chance and reveal a pressing problem. Incidentally, be ready for those famous four words soon after a red herring or smoke screen.

I remember that I would sometimes goof and do something like telling Carey to be sure to turn out all the lights. And I would then feel a swift kick under the covers, because my wife would recognize what the child was telling us and would know that she needed that precious commodity—focused attention. Always when we were on course, Carey continued the conversation on her own, talking initially about superficial things and gradually about items which were more and more important to her. After awhile, she would be sitting at the foot of our bed. Pretty soon she would be lying across the foot of the bed, the talk continuing to pour out. Before we knew it she would be lying between us. Finally, she would get to the thing which was bothering her. I remember one such time when she said, "I don't know if Jim likes me anymore. He's been so different." How difficult that was for Carey to come out with. She had to make sure the situation was safe for her to share. She had to put out her red herrings and smoke screens before she could finally reveal her problem.

Once a sensitive issue is out, it is a real temptation for parents to make light of it with a casual, seemingly flippant reply, as though it is such a trivial or easy-to-handle issue. We must take our teenagers seriously, examine their problems carefully with them, and help them to come to logical and sensible solutions. In this way, we not only will help them with their problems, but more importantly will cement our love-relationship with them.

And as we help them to solve their own problems, we can also be teaching them to think logically, rationally, and sequentially. Only by learning to think clearly can a teenager develop the ability to discern right from wrong and to develop a strong value system.

Guilt and Envy

To understand the background of most teenage problems, it is important to be aware of adolescent society. Teenage society is similar to the society of chickens—they both have a "pecking order," so to speak. The adolescent society is complex, but is based primarily on popularity and acceptance. It is important to know approximately where your child is in this network of relationships, because some of the most painful adolescent problems are peer-related and involve one or more of four feelings—envy, guilt, anger, and depression. Anger and depression will be discussed in detail later, so right now let's consider envy and guilt.

In dealing with peers, teenagers frequently have problems which naturally make them feel guilt or envy. Unfortunately, most teenagers are not good at identifying guilt or envy within themselves, and experience them as pain (distress) and/or confusion.

If a teenager's problem involves a peer who is lower on the adolescent society ladder, he will probably feel guilt. If his encounter was with someone above him, the feeling will usually be envy. When a conflict of interest or position arises, the teenager on the lower end, prompted by envy, will attempt to make the upper peer feel guilty.

It is important for parents to see their teenager's position in the conflict and identify the feelings the teenager is struggling with. Explaining the situation to a teenager will help him in several ways.

● It will enable him to understand exactly what is happening and *why*.

● It will help the teenager determine whether he has done anything wrong.

● It will assist him in handling this situation and others like it.

For example, if your teenager is feeling guilty, a clear understanding of the situation will usually reveal there is no blame to be laid and that the real problem is actually the other teenager's feeling of envy.

If your teenager is feeling envious, it is so helpful for him to be able to identify this within himself and to understand why. Then you will be in a position to help him correct the problem—by understanding that there is no real basis for the jealousy, if this is true, or by learning how to overcome the envy, if there *is* a basis for it.

When Carey won the Junior-Miss Pageant, nearly all of her peers were genuinely excited for her, and truly proud of her. But one evening, shortly afterward, Carey seemed troubled. As it turned out, an envious peer had made Carey feel guilty about winning the contest. The statement that produced the guilt was something like this: "Well, look at the big star! She sure thinks she's hot stuff!"

Carey felt miserable, typical of a teenager in this circumstance, and could not resolve her misery. Carey's mother helped her understand her feelings of guilt—that she had done nothing wrong, but was simply feeling a false guilt which had no basis.

Carey's experience illustrates the frequent problem of envy and guilt in the teenage world. It is vital to the emotional development of our teenagers that we help them to identify and understand envy and guilt in themselves, and learn how to handle these emotions properly. If they are unable to, they are likely to be *manipulated by guilt.*

Manipulation by Guilt

This is a great problem among adolescents today. The more sensitive a teenager is, the more susceptible he is to being manipulated by guilt. On the other hand, the less sensitive a teen is, the more apt he is to use this type of manipulation on others.

The maneuver is rather simple. Manipulator finds ways to make the manipulatee feel guilty if the manipulatee does not do what the manipulator wants. Of course, the classic example of this—and one of the most destructive—is the boy who attempts to induce a girl to have a sexual encounter with him with such remarks as, "If you really loved me, you would."

The parent of a sensitive teenager is in an excellent position to teach the child about this unwholesome device. The teenager needs to understand three things:

- how to recognize manipulation by guilt.

- that this device is unwholesome, unhealthy, and unethical—*that it is wrong.*

- that the normal and justifiable reaction to manipulation is *anger.*

In the story about the confrontation between Jesus and the money changers in the temple, I see manipulation as one element that caused Jesus' anger. The people coming to the temple needed to sacrifice to fulfill their religious obligation. They would feel guilty if they did not offer an animal sacrifice. In the scene which Jesus described as a cave full of robbers, there was manipulation by guilt. And Jesus' anger was an appropriate reaction. (See Matthew 21; Mark 11; Luke 19; John 2.)

I remember counseling a beautiful 16-year-old girl named Claudia. She was an extremely sensitive girl and in deep depression. During our conversation, I discovered that her boyfriend used guilt to manipulate her in many ways. As is so typical among teenagers, Claudia was not fully aware of her sensitivity, depression, or of being manipulated by guilt. First I explained to her how sensitive she was—how easy it was to hurt her and to make her feel guilty. Then I explained how others, especially her boyfriend, were able to control her by making her feel guilty if she didn't do what they wanted.

Because Claudia didn't understand at first what I was trying to tell her, I gave her an example that "wasn't so close to home." I said, "Claudia, I'm a sensitive person too, and I didn't learn how some people were able to manipulate me by guilt until a few years ago. After I finished medical school, I wanted to sell my house. I was having difficulty selling it myself, so I contracted a realtor to sell it for me. A few days later, a fellow medical student in my class who was going to remain in that city for an internship offered me a certain price for the home, but wanted to bypass the realtor and save the fees. I told him I could not do that—that he would have to go through the realtor. Later that day, the realtor came with an offer from another client and I took it. When my classmate found out that I had sold the house, he was furious and tried to talk me into changing my mind and selling it to him. The arguments that he used consisted of reminding me that we were fellow classmates, that I would make more money where I would be interning than he would make, and that the house had five years wear on it and was not worth the price the other person was offering."

Then I said. "Do you see, Claudia, how this man was trying to manipulate me into selling my house to him by making me feel guilty?"

Claudia's eyes lit up. She understood why she had so little control over her own life. The next time I saw Claudia her depression had lifted and there was a sparkle in her eye. She was learning how to think for herself and to determine her behavior rather than being manipulated by guilt.

Parents must be careful not to manipulate their teenagers by guilt. It is so easy for parents to fall into this trap, especially if they happen to have an extremely sensitive child. A teenager who has been manipulated with guilt by his own parents, will be easily manipulated by others.

What is the best way to prevent teenagers from being manipulated by guilt? Within the context of unconditional love and focused attention, parents can train their teenagers to identify manipulative behavior in others, and to stay free of its trap.

5

Eye Contact and Physical Contact

*Loving consistent eye contact with your
teenager is crucial.*

We live at a time in history when it is critical for our teenagers to feel and know that we really love them. There are unprecedented numbers of outside influences upon them, many of them unwholesome, and some of them evil and destructive. A teenager must feel genuinely loved to resist these influences. A teenager who does not feel loved and cared for is highly vulnerable to these influences. Many unscrupulous users of young people have seduced love-starved teenagers. By giving them time, attention, and affection, they have drawn these adolescents under their control.

The hour is late. As a parent, you have limited time and opportunities to make your teenager feel unconditionally loved. You must act today and be consistent every day in keeping his emotional tank full. This will enable him to grow into a person who can think competently and clearly for himself, and develop good self-control. Only when he truly feels that you unconditionally love and care for him will you have the influence on him that you should.

You want to tell him you love him. But you also want to show him your love in behavioral ways. We must emphasize this because most parents, although they deeply love their children, are not loving them *behaviorally*. Consequently, most of our young people today do not feel unconditionally and genuinely loved. This lack of feeling genuinely loved is at the bottom of most youth problems today. A child or teenager tends to follow the person whom he feels loves him the most.

Eye contact and physical contact should be incorporated into all of your everyday dealings with your children. They should be natural, comfortable, and not overdone. A child or teenager growing up in a home where parents use eye and physical contact will be comfortable with himself and with other people. He will have an easier time communicating with others, and consequently will be well-liked and feel high self-esteem.

Appropriate and frequent eye and physical contact are two of the most precious gifts you can give your teenager. They, along with focused attention, are the most effective ways to fill your teenager's emotional tank and enable him to be his best.

Eye Contact

One of the primary reasons loving parents fail to convey unconditional love to the teenager is lack of eye contact. Loving, consistent eye contact with your teenager is crucial not only in making good communicational contact, but also in filling his emotional needs. Without realizing it, you use eye contact to express many feelings—sadness, anger, hate, pity, rage, and love. In some homes, there is amazingly little eye contact between parents and teenagers. What exists is usually negative, as when the teenager is being reprimanded or given specific instructions. The more you are able to make eye contact with your teenager as a means of expressing love, the more your teenager will be emotionally nourished with love.

Your teenager will vary in his ability to make eye contact. One moment he will eagerly seek it. The next moment, he may actually avoid your gaze. Within this unevenness, he is learning patterns of eye contact, primarily from what he observes in his home from other members of the family.

Some time ago, I saw 17-year-old Bruce. Tall, well-built, and good-looking, he was an excellent student and athlete, and had a pleasant personality. Strangely enough, with all these things going for him, he had poor self-esteem and considered himself quite inadequate. It was easy to detect his low opinion of himself simply by observing his pattern of eye contact. His gaze was almost always downward. When he did make eye contact, it was for a fraction of a second. I explained to Bruce that the way he used eye contact strongly affected the way he related to other people. His poor pattern of eye contact actually worsened his self-concept. People felt uncomfortable with Bruce—they thought he didn't like them or was ignoring them. They were actually relieved to end a conversation and get away from him. Bruce naturally misinterpreted this as rejection and felt worse than ever. With a steady diet of this pattern over many years, it is no wonder Bruce developed a horrible misrepresentation of himself. Fortunately, it was simple to help Bruce correct his pattern of eye contact.

If your teenager has developed abnormal patterns of eye contact, you can teach him how he is misapplying it and how to correct it. Good eye contact can make the difference between success and failure in almost all of life's situations.

Giving loving eye contact to your teenager can be difficult, especially during those unpleasant times when he is noncommunicative. At times, a teenager can be very difficult to talk with, especially when he merely answers your questions with "uh-huh," "huh-uh," and similar grunts.

These unpleasant times of communication usually occur from one of three causes.

• The first is regression in psychosexual age, to be discussed in chapter 6. The teenager is resolving conflicts which have occurred in the past.

• The second is when the drive for independence is especially strong and the teenager feels a need to separate from the parents.

• The third is when the teenager has had an unpleasant experience with peers and feels hurt.

These periods of sullenness, withdrawal, and quietness are also usually accompanied by resistance to love and affection from parents.

During these times, it is a mistake to force yourself on your teenager, or prod him with questions. Often a parent will become irritated, worried, and even desperate, and try to open up conversation with persistent questions such as "How did your day go?"/"What happened to you today?"/"Did you have a good time?"/"Who was there?" This is irritating to anyone who is not in the mood to talk.

The secret is to *be available*. This means that instead of forcing interaction with your adolescent, you will be available at all times, so that he can communicate with you when he is comfortable in doing so.

As your child enters adolescence, he comes under increasing pressure from his drives for independence, sexual expressions, and peer acceptance. He must develop defenses against these pressures to prevent his being overwhelmed. Unfortunately, he occasionally uses rather primitive and unpleasant defenses such as retreating into states of withdrawal, noncommunication, and sullenness.

These primitive defenses cannot be penetrated or forced without damaging your relationship with the child. The only sensitive, sensible, and constructive way to manage these situations is to wait for the defenses to come down. You must *remain available* for your teenager to come to you when he is able.

However, there are definite things we can do to facilitate the lowering of these defenses, and we will discuss those later. But right now it is important to understand that attempting to batter down this extremely strong defense system is inadvisable.

The teenager's ability to use eye contact varies according to how strong this defense system is. When the teenager was younger, he was receptive of eye contact almost continuously. But as he enters into adolescence, there are uneasy periods when he is resistant to eye contact.

Do not let your teenager's occasional tendency to avoid eye

contact irritate you. Try simply to accept it, realizing if you remain available, he will come to you when his emotional tank is dry. At this time, he will be receptive of eye contact and will be communicative. It is important for his self-concept and psychological development for him to know that you will be available when he needs you.

Physical Contact

As a child becomes an adolescent, he needs continual reassurance from his parents that he is loved and accepted. The dilemma for many loving parents is their confusion as to how to meet this need.

Some parents attempt to do this by being overindulgent, providing their teens with things to keep up with their peers, like a car, stereo, or sporting equipment. These material things may be all right in themselves, but they are no substitute for what teenagers need most—unconditional love. Some parents use overindulgence by permitting, and many times even encouraging, their teenagers to go to places and do things which are not healthy for them. For example, I have known many parents who permit, and even encourage, their teens to go to parties which are designed to arouse sexual desires and where alcoholic beverages and other drugs are served. Few adolescents can handle such a situation, but this type of pressure on our youth is growing. Yet few parents are helping their teenagers to protect themselves from it. Few have enough influence on their teenagers to combat it. Why? Because they failed to make their teens feel that they are loved, accepted, and cared for.

Appropriate and consistent physical contact is a vital way to give your teenager that feeling and conviction that you truly care about him. This is especially true when your teenager is noncommunicative, sullen, moody, or resistant. During these times, eye contact may be difficult or even impossible. But physical contact can almost always be used effectively. Seldom does an adolescent respond negatively to a light, brief, touch on the shoulder, back, or arm. For example, suppose your teenager is just sitting in a chair watching TV. What a simple thing to briefly touch him on the shoulder as you walk by. Usually he will not even notice it, *but it registers* in his mind. You can use this vital information to give constant, consistent love by frequent, brief doses of physical contact. You can also use it by occasionally giving longer, more intense nurturance with more prolonged doses of physical contact.

Even when your teenager is in a noncommunicative mood, physical contact can be a means of conveying love to him. As long as your teenager's *focus of attention* is directed elsewhere, you are able to give prolonged physical contact *regardless* of the teenager's mood of receptiveness. For example, suppose your teenager is in an especially difficult state of mind that concerns you. You find an opportunity to talk with him about something which enables you to direct his attention *from himself,* to an object of interest, like pictures or photographs. You can really take advantage of such situations by putting your hand on his arm, shoulder, or back. You should know your teenager well enough to know how much physical contact he can accept at a particular time.

Sometimes your teenager will accept physical contact, but other times he may not be able to consciously tolerate your touch. At these times of nonacceptance, you can give physical contact when his attention is directed elsewhere so that he is *unaware* of the touch. Even when your teenager is not *consciously* aware of your physical contact, it registers. Its effect is to help him feel, "My mother and father love me and care for me, even during these times when relating to them is hard for me."

There are other ways to provide physical contact with a teenager. Frequently my 13-year-old David will strain or pull a muscle in a sport. He doesn't hesitate to ask me to massage the muscle for him. I am very grateful to do so, because this gives me a wonderful opportunity to use physical contact.

Once my daughter Carey landed the wrong way on a trampoline and her neck muscles needed rubbing. This was another good opportunity for physical contact.

Fortunately, all my children like to have their backs scratched. It's genuinely fun to scratch their backs. This has an amazing effect on their psychological defenses and also helps tremendously in keeping their emotional tanks full. Last summer when David came home from summer camp, what was the first thing he asked for? To have his back scratched, and to have his mother and me talk with him and read to him.

Although some parents are unwilling to provide emotional nurturance to their teenagers, especially with physical contact, I am very thankful that *most* parents love their young people enough to provide this for them. It is so simple to do, yet so wonderfully effective.

In certain situations, it is good to hug and kiss your teenager. Although you do not want to do it so often as to make him uncomfortable, there are times when it is appropriate: when departing or returning from a trip, or when the teenager does something of which *he* is especially proud—like winning an award. Or when your teenager comes to you feeling deeply hurt, remorseful, or otherwise troubled and seems to need it. And, of course, there are times when, for no discernible reason, your teenager simply feels a need for affection. If you are alert to provide it, what a special moment you will have with your child. *But* you must remain alert for such opportunities, because it is sometimes difficult to know when the teenager wants or needs affection.

Many times your teenager will be very subtle in *hinting* that he wants your attention or affection. He may approach you and talk about very superficial or meaningless topics. Usually, this is the key. At that moment, he seems so intense, serious, and persistent in mood, and very much out of context, considering the topic of conversation. At such a time, it is important to be patient. Your teenager is buying time in your presence until his psychological defenses have time to come down enough so that he can talk about important and meaningful things. Be very careful not to be in a hurry and cut off the communication. Your teenager would naturally interpret this as rejection and your relationship with him might be harmed. If you are patient and give your teenager the time he needs, his superficial conversation will eventually give way to what he really wants to talk about. You must be an active listener, and this requires patience.

At family conferences, one of the most common questions parents ask me is this: "If I have given my teenager very little eye contact and physical contact, how can I make up for it?" This is a very good question. Such parents should not overwhelm their teenagers by suddenly giving large amounts of eye and physical contact. First, they need to obtain a baseline—a general idea of how much eye and physical contact their teenagers can accept. Starting from there, they will *gradually* increase contact over the next weeks and months. The less noticeable the increases are, the better, and the more comfortable the teenagers will be.

Someone has said, "Thank goodness adolescence is a time-limited disease." We parents need to hang in there during this period of difficult and intense change. The more we maintain our cool and self-control, the smoother and less traumatic the time will be. Our children will emerge from the teenage years more mature, and our relationships with them will be better when they reach adulthood.

When we remain available to give our teenagers the love they need whenever they can accept it, we are demonstrating the manner in which God relates to us. He is constantly available to nurture and help us, as members of His family, even when we are rejecting of Him. "If we are unfaithful to Him, He Himself will remain faithful" (2 Timothy 2:13).

6

Parental Self-Control

*Emotional overreaction
is destructive if it happens too often.*

Mr. and Mrs. Oliver looked at each other and shook their heads in puzzlement. Not 10 minutes before, their 16-year-old daughter, Amy, was explaining precisely how she managed to land a much-sought-after position, by impressing the employer with how mature she was. Now, she was crying uncontrollably because her brother had used her shampoo.

Parents of teenagers know that adolescence is a tumultuous time in which the teenage child can swing from toddler to adult, from sweet to sour, from logical to irrational, and back again, all within the span of a day or an hour. These changes can be intense and frequent, and too few parents know exactly why they happen.

In the teenage years, young people are attempting to resolve all conflicts they have previously experienced in their lives, especially with their parents. Although teenagers are not conscious of this desire to resolve old conflicts, the drive within them to do so is so strong that it appears to others that the teenagers have chosen a deliberate course of action.

For this reason, an early adolescent between the ages of 12 and 15 will evidence frequent and unexpected mood shifts. One minute he will seem to be very mature, and the next minute like a small child. Before he can comfortably and normally grow away from his parents and become responsibly independent, a teenager must clear his past, so to speak, of problems and conflicts he has had with people, and especially with his parents.

When my daughter Carey was 13, I noticed one day that her attitude toward me was one of irritability and some hostility. I asked her, "Please tell me, Honey, have I done anything that has upset or hurt you?" Without hesitation she recounted an incident that occurred six years previously. We were riding in a station wagon; my wife and I were in the front seat, the other children in the middle seat, and Carey with a friend in the back seat. All the kids were throwing popcorn at each other. Because it was distracting me as I was driving, I yelled for them to stop. Carey exclaimed that I had embarrassed her, by "screaming at her friends." Yes, I remembered the incident but never guessed that it had affected her so deeply.

At that moment Carey had psychologically regressed to a seven-year-old level in order to deal with that particular conflict. After she revealed this encounter to me (and I noted the anger in her voice), I told her that I honestly had not realized the embarrassment and pain I had caused her. When I told her I was sorry and asked her forgiveness, she was immediately relieved and became her 13-year-old self again.

This regression and advance in psychological age is one reason why early teenagers are so unpredictable and sometimes difficult to understand. Parents should react to them according to the age they are exhibiting at that time. For instance, let's say your early adolescent approaches you with a highly sophisticated statement such as, "Dad, what do you think of the Middle East crisis? I wonder if the displaced Palestinian Arab families should be entitled to return to their homes and be a normal part of the Israeli nation." After a couple of gulps, you are able to communicate with him on that exact level and discuss the issue.

But that same teenager may be back 30 minutes later with what appears to be a two-year-old temper tantrum. What do you do? Right! Relate to him as would be appropriate with a two-year-old having a temper tantrum. As you can easily see, this takes real flexibility on your part to change your level of communication rapidly. This is why a good, flexible youth counselor, who is dealing with several early adolescents, can be utterly exhausted at the end of the day.

It is extremely important that you as parents exhibit emotional self-control. Emotional overreaction will hurt your relationship with your teenager in several ways.

• Excessive and uncontrolled anger will make it difficult for your teenager to come to you when his emotional tank needs refilling.

• Emotional overreaction tends to cause your adolescent to respect you less—a very natural response to anyone who lacks self-control.

• Losing your cool tends to push your teen into the influence of others, especially peers.

Maintaining Self-Control

But how do you keep yourself in good condition emotionally? How do you maintain self-control? The most common problems which adversely affect an adult's ability to control anger are depression, fatigue, and anxiety. Most people are ineffective in preventing depression because they do not realize how closely it is related to how much time they spend with people and how much time they spend alone. In other words, time balance. Each person has a different need in this regard. Some require more time socially relating to people than others, while some require more time alone. Unfortunately, I cannot think of one person I have come across who was actually aware of this crucial fact. Most people follow this pattern: they find themselves spending more and more time with people, to the point of social saturation. They become more prone to depression because they are emotionally drained and fatigued from the excessive social contact. Depression causes most people to want to withdraw and become seclusive. This, along with being tired of being around people, causes them to spend too much time alone. But then they feel lonely, yearn to be with people, seek them out, and the cycle starts again. This is one reason few people lead balanced, well-adjusted lives.

Of course, some unfortunate people do not have enough control over their lives to achieve this balance. They may be forced to spend too much time with people because they do not have the means to privacy. Others spend too much time alone, because they are old, ill, or do not have access to friends. Either way, depression is usually miserably present.

For the sake of your own mental health and for that of your teenager, you need to determine what percentage of your time should be spent with people, and how much should be spent alone. This differs from every person and your own ratio can change with times and seasons and circumstances.

The quality of each kind of time is important also, especially the time alone, which should be emotionally refreshing for you. This may mean reading a good book, hiking, walking, exercising alone, praying, or meditating. Television seldom fills this need. In fact, TV seems to leave most people even more emotionally drained.

Emotional stability and self-control do not just happen. You must prepare yourself to cope with emotional strain and frustration. A normal teenager will bring forth both. To maintain a healthy relationship with your teenager and keep communications open, you need to be in good control of yourself, especially of your anger. Emotional overreaction is destructive if it happens too often and is not resolved. We all overreact at times, and if we don't do it too often, it is possible to produce a positive situation out of a negative one. This may involve apologizing to a son or daughter for overreacting and asking for forgiveness: "Honey, I'm sorry I overdid it and yelled yesterday. What you did was wrong, but I overreacted and should have handled it in a calmer way. Will you forgive me?" This approach not only prevents many disasters, but can actually strengthen and sweeten a parent-teenager relationship. However, if you overreact too often or in extreme ways, simply saying you're sorry and asking forgiveness will not work; it could even lower you in your child's eyes.

The more pleasant you are with your teenager, the firmer you can afford to be in setting limits and in discipline. Likewise, the more unpleasant you are with your teenager, the less firm you can afford to be. Why? First of all, as we have already stated, the more unpleasant you are, the less your teenager will respect you and the more he will be inclined to go against your wishes. Second, the more unpleasant you are, the more parental authority you have dissipated in ventilating your own anger and frustration. The more pleasant you are, the more parental authority you have saved to control your teenager's behavior. And this is what you want, good behavior control! How can you really expect good self-control from your teenager if you do not have it yourself? Energy, preparation, self-discipline, and self-control are needed if you are going to be pleasant in the midst of unpleasant but normal adolescent strivings.

Anger is difficult to control if your *spiritual* life is not sound. An unhealthy spiritual life can cause depression and anxiety. It can also affect your thought control in such a way that you arrive at wrong decisions or conclusions—including your ideas regarding other people's motives. Any of these problems can make you lose spiritual perspective and can hinder your ability to control anger.

I believe a healthy spiritual life is one in which communications are open between you and God. How is this done? First, make sure you have a clean heart, by asking God to search your heart and convict you of any wrong He finds there. Next, confess these wrongs and obtain God's forgiveness and cleansing. This clears the channel of communication between you and God. Now you are ready to draw close to Him and He to you. God is then able to fill your emotional and spiritual tank. He does this by being with you, close to you, listening, guiding, comforting, and reassuring you with His promises and love.

It takes time to fellowship with God long enough to really know Him and long enough for Him to fill you and prepare you for your responsibilities as a parent.

I find it very difficult to spend time alone with God, without distractions. My time for emotional and spiritual refreshment with my heavenly Father often happens after all the kids are in bed, usually between 9 and 9:30 at night. To escape distractions, I often take a walk or just sit outside, weather permitting, or in a quiet room. It usually takes 10-20 minutes of solitude to feel close to God, to quiet my inner self after a typically hectic day. God doesn't hurry or rush. He is so calm and He continues to speak in a still, small voice.

Your ability to handle anger is influenced by many things, most of which have little or nothing to do with your teenager. One of these is your physical condition. Are you eating foods that will help you feel your best? I have seen so many people who believe their diets are healthy, when in actuality they are not. Most authorities consider breakfast the most important meal of the day. What you eat for breakfast pretty well determines how you feel the rest of the day. Most people eat too much carbohydrate and not enough protein and bulk for breakfast. This usually produces a lack of energy later and induces them to seek stimulants such as coffee or soft drinks (many soft drinks have caffeine in them). Caffeine has differing effects on people, but none of them aid the emotional stability and calmness you need with your teenager. Therefore, a healthy, low carbohydrate breakfast with plenty of protein and bulk, and avoidance of caffeine is a good start in gaining self-control.

Many people believe that they are doing themselves a favor by skipping breakfast or even lunch. Skipping meals does not aid in weight reduction or promote a sense of well-being. For lunch, it is important not to eat too much carbohydrate, and to avoid caffeine. Excessive carbohydrate will sap energy. Caffeine will increase irritability. It is amazing how much better I feel from lunch to supper on a green salad rather than a sandwich or hamburger.

Supper is the meal at which most people tend to overeat. This is one reason why a healthy breakfast and lunch are important. If you have had too much carbohydrate or have skipped breakfast or lunch, you may not be able to control your dietary intake later in the day, especially in the midst of depression or fear. And, of course, if you eat improperly at these times, you will not feel your best during the evening.

Employing good common sense—a regular exercise program, good diet, recreation, a healthy spiritual life—can go a long way toward preventing depression. Unfortunately, not all depression can be prevented. Many people are biochemically or hereditarily prone to depression. If a person has done all in his power to prevent depression, yet becomes depressed, he should seek help—not only for his own sake, but also for the sake of his family. A moderately to severely depressed parent simply cannot handle a normal teenager well. The relationship between parent and child will suffer, and so will the teenager himself.

Bob

Bob was a 17-year-old boy whom I saw because of drug usage, poor grades, and a defiant attitude. When I saw him alone, he was a calm, polite boy, and exceptionally easy to communicate with. I felt he was truthful when he stated that he did not like his behavior and wanted to change. He said that he had been trying to make a change in his behavior. But after bouts of fighting and arguing with his father—which were daily occurrences—he would become so angry that all he could think of was getting back by doing the very things his father (and Bob) did not like. Of course, I wanted to check out Bob's perceptions and see if they were accurate. So I asked Bob's parents to join us.

Bob's father was an extraordinarily angry man. He immediately made a grossly hostile remark about Bob's "terrible and unacceptable behavior." His anger and the ferocity of his remarks continued and even increased. Bob made no response but deep, painful anger was obviously welling up inside him. Finally, Bob's mother tried to intervene by telling the father that Bob's behavior had been good recently and that she could not understand why he was so angry. Also, I noticed that the behavior about which the father was complaining did not justify such vehement condemnation. The father not only ignored the mother's pleas, but used

Bob's behavior as an excuse to rid himself of excessive anger. When I talked to the father alone, I learned the real cause of his frustration. He was having severe problems at work, was extremely depressed, could not sleep well, could hardly eat, tired easily, and felt life was not worth living. Bob was the only "safe" place to ventilate his misery. I don't know which one made my heart ache most—Bob, his mother, or his father.

It is a common thing for teenagers to be receptacles of parents' displaced anger. Teenagers often tend to put pressure on us, make us tense, upset, and angry. Therefore it sometimes seems justifiable to dump all accumulated anger on them. This is so dangerous! Excessive and overreactive anger is an enemy of parents seeking to relate to their teenagers. Nothing else cuts off parent-adolescent communications the way poorly controlled anger does.

Most parents seem to assume that their teenagers do not need their love and affection as they did as small children. This is simply not true. Teenagers continue to need love, affection, assurance, and care as never before, even though in their biological drive for independence, they may sometimes act as though they don't.

I made that mistake with my daughter Carey. Her 18th birthday and graduation from high school occurred at about the same time. In my mind I unconsciously graduated her from being my child to an independent adult. Fortunately, my wife, Pat, noticed the effect of this. I was not as loving or caring with Carey as before; this hurt her because she felt that she had done something wrong. Pat told me about this and, thank goodness, I was able to again relate to her as a daughter—as my child.

We never really grow out of the need to be loved and cared for. These needs may be gradually taken over by other people in adult life. But during the years when our children are dependent on us, we parents must always stand available and ready to love and nourish them whenever we're needed, especially during the teenage years.

71

7

Teenage Anger

You can make me go to school but you can't make me get good exam results.

Many parents assume that anger in a child is bad or abnormal, and that expression of it should be suppressed or not allowed. This is a dangerous error. We are instructed in Scripture to "train up a child in the way he should go," to educate him "according to his life requirements" (Proverbs 22:6, KJV and MLB). One of the most important areas in which a child, especially a teenager, needs training is in how to handle anger.

The feeling of anger is not bad or good in itself. Anger is normal and occurs in every human being. The problem is not the anger itself but in managing it. And this is where most people have problems. I believe it is *imperative* to understand the different ways to handle anger, and to know which ways are better or worse.

Passive-Aggressive Behavior

Let's start with what I consider the absolutely worst way to handle anger—*passive-aggressive behavior*. I generally avoid using professional terms, but this is one term I strongly recommend your knowing. Passive-aggressive behavior is the opposite of an open, honest, direct, and verbal expression of anger. Passive-aggressive behavior is an expression of anger that gets back at a person indirectly. A few examples of this are procrastination, dawdling, stubbornness, intentional inefficiency, and "forgetfulness." The subconscious purpose of passive-aggressive behavior is to *upset* the parents or parent figures and to make them angry.

Passive-aggressive techniques of handling anger are indirect, cunning, self-defeating, and destructive. Unfortunately, passive-aggressive behavior is subconsciously motivated; that is, the child is not consciously aware that he is using this resistant, obstructive behavior to release his pent-up anger to upset his parents.

One of the earliest ways a child can show passive-aggressive tendencies is by soiling his pants, after he has been toilet-trained. In many such cases, the parents have prohibited the child from expressing any anger, especially verbally. Then, if the parents have overreacted by becoming excessively angry or even punishing him whenever he expresses his anger openly, what can the child do with his normally occurring anger?

A child in this situation may use passive-aggressive behavior to get back at the parents in ways which will upset them, like soiling his pants—a very effective but unhealthy way to express anger. You know that there's little the parents can do in such a situation. Because they have refused to permit the child to openly and directly express anger, the child has been forced to use an indirect, harmful way to do it, and the parents have backed themselves into a corner. The more the parents punish the child, the more he will soil his pants. Why? Because the subconscious purpose of passive-aggressive behavior is to *upset* the parents. What a dilemma! God pity both parent and child in such a situation.

Many older children who use passive-aggressive means to express anger do very poor work in school. Their attitude is, "You can lead a horse to water, but you can't make him drink. You can make me go to school, but you can't make me get good grades." Again, the parents are helpless, the children's anger is in control. The more the parents become upset—the subconscious purpose of all this—the worse the situation becomes.

It is important to know that the passive-aggressive child does not do these things consciously or purposefully. They are part of an unconscious process of which he is not aware, and into which he has been forced by his parents.

Passive-aggressive behavior in younger children is bad enough, but passive-aggressive behavior in teenagers can be utterly disastrous. I have seen this unhealthy way of handling anger cause teenagers to run the gamut—from making poor grades to using drugs, becoming pregnant, committing crimes, and attempting suicide. There are, of course, other causes for these types of behavior. The passive-aggressive tendency, however, is a most serious cause that is on the increase among teenagers.

I have seen many teenagers who do poorly in school because their parents have made themselves unapproachable—either by their own emotional overreaction or by being intolerant in not allowing their teenagers to express negative or unpleasant feelings. I have seen teenagers who break parental rules, including coming in habitually late, not because of a normal drive for independence, but as a way to upset their parents and express their anger indirectly. I have seen girls who got pregnant as an act of anger toward parents because they were never allowed to express unpleasant feelings, especially anger. I have seen teenagers who developed antisocial and antiauthority attitudes as means to express anger.

More complexly, I have seen teenagers turn their unresolved anger onto themselves to cause psychosomatic problems such as headaches, ulcers, and skin problems. And most tragically, I have seen this passive-aggressive behavior so ingrained in teenagers that it becomes their primary way of handling any anger-provoking situation which may confront them, even to the point of committing suicide as a means to indirectly express anger.

Recently I saw a 16-year-old girl whose parents mistakenly thought they were raising their daughter correctly by refusing to allow her to express any unpleasant feelings, especially anger. They thought they would teach her to be a happy person by learning to express only pleasant feelings. She learned to avoid open expression of her anger to the source of her frustration; she would habitually express her anger in ways which would indirectly hurt the person who caused her anger. This became such a habit that most of her behavior was understandable only by knowing that she was trying to hurt someone indirectly. What finally brought her to seek help was her sixth suicide attempt. Each of the attempts was planned to make a particular person feel guilty, upset, and hurt. The first five attempts were half-hearted and no great threat to her life. However, the sixth resulted in her being in a coma and near death for several days. As I talked with her after she recovered, I saw that her conduct definitely puzzled her. She did not understand that her behavior was a long-established pattern of expressing anger in unhealthy, self-defeating, destructive, indirect, and displaced ways.

Passive-aggressive behavior is very common. Why? Because most people do not understand anger or know what to do with it. They feel that anger is somehow wrong or sinful and should be "disciplined" out of the child. This is a serious misunderstanding, because the feeling of anger is normal and has been encountered by every person who has ever been born. If when your child becomes angry and you spank him, or yell at him: "Stop that kind of talk. I will not allow it!" what can the child do? Only two things—he can disobey you and continue to "talk that way," or obey you and "stop talking that way." If he chooses the latter and ceases to express his anger,the anger will not go away. The child will simply suppress the anger into his subconscious, where it will remain unresolved and waiting to be expressed later through inappropriate and/or passive-aggressive behavior.

Another mistake some parents make, related to expression of anger, is the inappropriate use of humor. Whenever a situation becomes tense, especially if someone is becoming angry, many parents will interject humor to relieve the tension. Of course, humor is a wonderful asset in any family. But where it is consistently used to escape the appropriate handling of anger, teenagers simply cannot learn how to appropriately deal with it.

I recently visited a family where the father had an uncommonly humorous wit. Whenever his wife or one of his teenagers began expressing an unpleasant feeling, he would come up with an hilarious statement. Consequently, none of the teenagers in that family could deal with anger and resorted to passive-aggressive means of expressing it indirectly. Whenever the boy would experience frustration or anger-provoking situations, he would have severe headaches. The girl manifested her anger indirectly by voluntarily helping her mother with housework, but doing such a poor job that she often caused the mother more work than if she had not helped at all.

Passive-aggressive behavior easily becomes an ingrained, habitual pattern which can last a lifetime. If a child or teenager avoids honestly and openly dealing with anger in an appropriate manner, he may use passive-aggressive techniques in every relationship. This can affect his relationships later with spouse, children, work associates, and friends. What a tragedy! And most of these unfortunate people are not fully aware of their self-defeating patterns of behavior or their problems with handling anger.

Incidentally, one of the most common and dangerous types of passive-aggressiveness is seen in driving habits. Have you ever noticed how some people speed up when you try to pass them? Or the driver on the highway who passes you and then darts in front of you, forcing you to use your brakes to avoid running into him? These are blatant examples of passive-aggressive behavior. Needless to say it is difficult to appreciate a passive-aggressive person.

This brings to mind a 39-year-old woman named Margaret. She was born and raised in a Christian home. Unfortunately, her parents believed that a child should not be permitted to express anger. So she was never trained in how to properly handle or resolve it. Consequently she developed into an individual whose overall behavior pattern was designed to upset her parents. Her whole life was aimed at doing the exact opposite of what her parents would want. Her behavior patterns are unconscious, or out of her awareness. Consciously, she thinks of herself as a well-meaning Christian who earnestly desires to live a proper lifestyle. However, she has had one affair after another with married men. She has been indicted for embezzlement and fraud.

Margaret is an enigma to herself. Until therapy, she could not understand why her lifestyle and behavioral patterns were entirely inconsistent with her basic beliefs. Hers is a wasted life of self-abasement and self-destruction, because her primary purpose in living is to behave in ways which are just the opposite of what her parents would want her to be. Tragic!

Passive-aggressive behavior is absolutely the worst way to express anger for several reasons.

● It can easily become an ingrained tenacious pattern of behavior which will last a lifetime.

● It can distort a person's personality and make him a quite disagreeable person.

● It can interfere in all the teenager's future relationships.

● It is one of the most difficult behavioral disorders to treat and correct.

Scripture instructs us to train a child in the way he should go. Forcing a child to suppress the anger and not to deal with it properly is training him in the way he should *not* go. It is crucial to train a child in the proper way to handle anger. This is done by teaching him to resolve the anger, not to suppress it.

The Anger Ladder

There are many ways to express anger. The more immature a person is, the more immaturely he will express his anger. The more mature he is, the more maturely he will express his anger. Handling anger appropriately and maturely is one of the most difficult lessons in becoming a mature person, one that many adults never learn.

Children will tend to express anger immaturely, until *trained* to do otherwise. A teenager cannot be expected to *automatically* express his anger in the best, most mature way. But this is what parents are expecting, when they simply tell their teen not to get mad. Parents must train teenagers to take one step at a time in learning to deal with anger.

The Anger Ladder is designed to illustrate the different steps or levels of maturity in expressing anger, and to help parents see that a teenager must be trained to progress from one rung or level of maturity to the next, as he expresses his anger more and more appropriately.

1. As we discussed before, passive-aggressive behavior is the worst way to express anger.

2. A slightly better way to express anger is to be utterly *out of control behaviorally* in such a way that the person is in a fit of rage, actually destroys property, and/or is violent toward another person. As bad as this may sound, passive-aggressive behavior is worse. Why? Because rageous behavior is much easier to deal with, correct, and prevent than passive-aggressive behavior.

3. A somewhat better way to express anger is to be in a *fit of rage,* but maintaining enough self-control to prevent property destruction and personal violence. The outburst is confined to yelling, screaming, or cursing in such a way as to verbally hurt someone, perhaps with name-calling or accusatory remarks. The anger is expressed not only at the person with whom we are angry, but at anyone who happens to be in the vicinity. As poor and immature as these methods are in expressing anger, they are far better than passive-aggressive behavior or other ways of displaying anger behaviorally.

4. The next better way to handle anger is uncontrollably ventilating it *verbally* but without seeking to hurt anyone verbally, as with name-calling or criticizing. In this situation the anger is directed not only toward the source of the anger but toward anyone who happens to be around. As primitive and poor as this method is, it is better than any we have mentioned yet.

5. A somewhat better way to handle anger is to ventilate it unpleasantly, perhaps by yelling and screaming, but confining the remarks to the provoking issue, and, if possible, toward the person provoking the anger. Of course, whether expressing the anger toward the person who has angered the teenager is appropriate or not depends on the particular situation.

6. The best way to express anger is to do it as pleasantly and rationally as possible, and toward the person one is angry at. You hope that the person receiving the anger will respond in an equally

mature way, attempt to understand the other's position, and that the two can resolve the issue. Resolving the issue means for both parties to rationally and logically examine the issue, discuss it, understand it from both points of view, and to come to an agreement on what to do about it. This takes a great deal of maturity on both sides. Few people ever come to this point of maturity in their lives.

I have found that describing the different levels of maturity in expressing anger becomes very complex and difficult to understand. To simplify it as much as possible and yet give you a workable knowledge of it, I have created an Anger Ladder.

The list of 15 ways of behaving while angry are combined in various arrangements on the Anger Ladder. Notice that most expressions of anger are primarily negative. On the ladder, only the top two rungs are totally positive.

1. Pleasant behavior
2. Seeking resolution
3. Focusing anger on source only
4. Holding to the primary complaint
5. Thinking logically and constructively
6. Unpleasant and loud behavior
7. Cursing
8. Displacing anger to sources other than the original
9. Expressing unrelated complaints
10. Throwing objects
11. Destroying property
12. Verbal abuse
13. Emotionally destructive behavior
14. Physical abuse
15. Passive-aggressive behavior

Each rung on the Anger Ladder represents a progressively better way to express anger. You want to train your child to take one step at a time, to go up one rung at a time. How do you do this?

POSITIVE

1. PLEASANT ● SEEKING RESOLUTION ● FOCUSING ANGER ON SOURCE ● HOLDING TO PRIMARY COMPLAINT ● THINKING LOGICALLY
2. PLEASANT ● FOCUSING ANGER ON SOURCE ● HOLDING TO PRIMARY COMPLAINT ● THINKING LOGICALLY

POSITIVE and NEGATIVE

3. FOCUSING ANGER ON SOURCE ● HOLDING TO PRIMARY COMPLAINT ● THINKING LOGICALLY ● unpleasant, loud
4. HOLDING TO PRIMARY COMPLAINT ● THINKING LOGICALLY ● unpleasant, loud ● displacing anger to other sources
5. FOCUSING ANGER ON SOURCE ● HOLDING TO PRIMARY COMPLAINT ● THINKING LOGICALLY ● unpleasant, loud ● verbal abuse
6. HOLDING TO PRIMARY COMPLAINT ● THINKING LOGICALLY ● unpleasant, loud ● displacing anger to other sources
7. THINKING LOGICALLY ● unpleasant, loud ● displacing anger to other sources ● expressing unrelated complaints

PRIMARILY NEGATIVE

8. unpleasant, loud ● displacing anger to other sources ● expressing unrelated complaints ● emotionally destructive behavior
9. unpleasant, loud ● displacing anger to other sources ● expressing unrelated complaints ● verbal abuse ● emotionally destructive behavior
10. unpleasant, loud ● cursing ● displacing anger to other sources ● expressing unrelated complaints ● verbal abuse ● emotionally destructive behavior
11. FOCUSING ANGER ON SOURCE ● unpleasant, loud ● cursing ● throwing objects ● emotionally destructive behavior
12. unpleasant, loud ● cursing ● displacing anger to other sources ● throwing objects ● emotionally destructive behavior

NEGATIVE

13. FOCUSING ANGER ON SOURCE ● unpleasant, loud ● cursing ● destroying property ● verbal abuse ● emotionally destructive behavior
14. unpleasant, loud ● cursing ● displacing anger to other sources ● destroying property ● verbal abuse ● emotionally destructive behavior
15. unpleasant, loud ● cursing ● displacing anger to other sources ● destroying property ● verbal abuse ● physical abuse ● emotionally destructive behavior
16. passive = aggressive behavior

As parents, you should be good examples in the proper expression of anger. Also, you can expect your teenager to become angry at times. Instead of forbidding him to become angry or overreacting to his anger, you need to meet him where he is in his handling of anger and train him from there. For example, one teenager handles anger at the level of rung 6 on the Anger Ladder. That is, he is unpleasant about it, expresses it at inappropriate people (for example, his little brother instead of the person at whom he is angry), he sticks to the primary complaint only (that is, only what is bothering him), and he is logical and constructive (he is trying to make things better, not worse).

You then determine what improvement you want for your teenager. In this example, you want him to learn to direct his anger to the appropriate person and *not* take it out on his younger brother.

To train him, you should find a time soon after you both have calmed down and the atmosphere is pleasant. At this best of possible moments, compliment and praise your teenager in the areas of expressing his anger which he did *correctly*. *Then* ask your teenager to correct that one selected aspect which you want changed—in this case, taking his anger out on his younger brother.

Let me clarify one point of possible confusion. It is in *verbal* expression of anger that you need to train your teenager, so that he learns to handle it better. I am not encouraging permissiveness in behavior. You must remain firm in not allowing your teenager to behave inappropriately. Limit-setting regarding behavior must be firm and consistent. This distinction between verbal and behavioral expressions of anger is critical.

David

Like most people, I have my moments when anger is a problem for me—anger within me and anger in my children. However, here is one experience which I believe I handled correctly. And, best of all, I gained tremendous insight into the whole area of a child's anger. My 13-year-old David was overloaded with homework one day. He arrived home at about 3:30 that afternoon, and except for

10 minutes for supper, was still working on academics at 11:30 that night. He also had a book report due in a few days. At 11:30 I said, "David, I don't care how much homework you still have to do, you need your sleep and I want you in bed now."

He replied, "Please give me five more minutes, Dad, I'm almost finished."

I said, "OK, five more minutes and that's it."

I then returned to my bedroom with my wife. In a few minutes, David came into the room with a book in his hand, walked up to his mother, and said, "Mom, I think I'll use this book for my book report."

His mother looked at the book and replied, "No, David, you can't use that book because it's the same one you used last year."

David said, "I know, but I can make another book report on it and won't have to read a new book."

"I'm sorry, David," his mother replied, "that wouldn't be right. You have to read another book."

David got mad and answered his mother in a loud, angry voice, "OK, I'll read it. Just help me find another book and I'll read it. OK, I'll read another book!"

My first reaction was a typical one toward a child who was verbally ventilating anger in an unpleasant, loud way—I felt the anger rising within me. My first thought was, *How dare he talk to his mother that way! I'll show him that he can't get away with being nasty like that.*

But, fortunately, I remembered a previous event. Three days before, I became so infuriated at a man (and at church, mind you!) that I called him a liar. Who handled his anger better? David or I? Then I realized that David had managed his anger better than I had and that he was on rung 3 on the Anger Ladder. I was near rung 5. He directed his anger at its source—his mother. He didn't take it out on his little brother, kick his dog, destroy property, attempt to hurt his mother with names or criticism, or use passive-aggressive behavior. He didn't bring up unpleasant subjects or previous grievances. He simply stated that he would read another book. Who can improve on that? The only thing David did wrong was to speak loudly to his mother. Not many people, mature adults included, can beat that.

Now what would have happened if I had lit into David and punished him? I'll tell you. Because he was on rung 3 of the Anger Ladder, the *next* time he got angry, he would have been forced to use a more immature way of expressing his anger at a lower level on the Anger Ladder.

Then what should I do? The best thing for me to do at that time was to not respond. Not responding does *not* mean condoning. By the look on my face and on his mother's face, he knew we didn't like what he was doing. By *not responding* we were telling David, "We don't like what you are doing, but if you choose to do so, go ahead. It is not bad enough to stop, but we don't like it."

After we all calmed down, David went to bed. During our usual nighttime ritual (here's a good example where nighttime rituals pay off), and after we had prayed together, I said to David, "I was very proud of the way you handled your anger tonight. You didn't take it out on your brother or the dog. You didn't throw anything, or sulk, or say anything wrong. You spoke directly to your mother without trying to hurt her with names or criticism. You simply said you would read another book. That's great. The only thing you did wrong was to yell at your mother." The effect was great. David felt relieved that I wasn't angry with him but also felt very bad about yelling at his mother. The next day he apologized to her.

Train Your Teenager

When your teenager expresses anger directly, be glad. The more he uses verbalizations to express his anger, the better it is. Then determine where your teen is functioning on the Anger Ladder. Determine in what ways he is expressing anger appropriately and in what ways he is being inappropriate.

You want to *train* your teen in the way he should go. First, praise him for appropriate ways he is expressing anger. Then you can talk to him about *one of the inappropriate ways* he is using (like name-calling), asking him to correct it. You want to choose the best possible moment; then talk to your teenager about correcting one item at a time. You are *training* your child to gradually go up the Anger Ladder *one rung at a time*.

Most parents expect their children to handle anger maturely, at the highest rung, *with no training*. This is like saying to a tennis student before his first lesson, "I believe you should be about ready for the Wimbledon by now."

In some cases, it is impossible to resolve anger, as for example, when the person provoking the anger is inaccessible. At these times, the teenager must learn other appropriate ways to ventilate the anger, like exercise, talking it over with a mature person, using diversion such as an enjoyable activity, or spending time alone in a relaxed manner.

Another way to train a teenager in handling his own anger is to teach the art of preventing certain types of anger *cognitively*. This means using active intellectual reasoning to reduce the anger. For example, I've seen a wonderful change in my 13-year-old boy's ability to control anger in the last year. Instead of strictly reacting emotionally, he has learned to use his thought processes more.

A year ago David occasionally lost his temper when playing baseball if another player did something which was obviously wrong, especially if it resulted in physical pain to David. But last summer, I noticed a degree of progress. For example, in one game David was running from third base to home plate when the catcher caught the throw from the outfield. He was ready to tag David out when David suddenly surprised the catcher by jumping over his glove. Unfortunately in doing this he also jumped over home plate. He was on his stomach reaching back to touch the plate when the catcher, infuriated at being tricked, hit David in the face while tagging him. I was stunned and was afraid that David, being the larger boy, would overreact with violence. Much to my relief and amazement, he just dusted himself off and calmly walked to the dugout. David had learned to intellectually nip the anger in the bud by realizing that this particular player had difficulty handling anger and would express it inappropriately. In short, David knew that the catcher did not have anything against him personally and had acted this way because of his own problems with behavior.

Most adults handle their strong anger in inappropriate ways. They may lose control of themselves and ventilate their anger toward the wrong person. They may hurt the persons at whom they are angry behind their backs, by using passive-aggressive behavior in some indirect and immature way. Why? Because no one trained them in the better ways to handle anger. Who failed to train them? Their parents.

However, at this point we must be aware that some children are more naturally prone to have difficulties handling anger than others—regardless of the type of parenting they have had. For example, children and teenagers with certain neurological problems are especially prone to handling anger in passive-aggressive ways. This is especially true and quite frequent if there is a history of perceptual or learning problems. These children and teenagers (and later adults) tend to have problems with passive aggressive behavior and depression.

You see immature ways of handling anger every day. You see a wife and husband yelling, screaming, and cursing at each other. You see the wife or husband having an affair to get back at the other. You see an employee doing poor work to undermine the employer's interests. You see a principal abusing a teacher. You see a teacher subtly working against a principal. You see special interest groups attempting to materially hurt others. Immature handling of anger is on every hand. It is one of the greatest problems in business today, resulting in poor attitudes in employer and employee alike. Sixty to eighty percent of problems in any organization are personnel related, because so few people learned how to deal with anger maturely. Most are very good at hiding it superficially, when dealing face to face with others; but out it comes later, in inappropriate ways.

One of the most important things to understand about anger, whether we are dealing with employees, unions, government, or teenagers, is that it is bound to occur. It can result from any human interaction. The next important fact is that it will tend to build up and become more and more difficult to control, even explosive, if not dealt with. And the more difficult it is to control, the more destructive it may become. Therefore, we must find ways to either "nip it in the bud" if the anger is based on misunderstanding, or to see that the anger is ventilated slowly and then resolved, if it is justified. Such control does not come naturally to anyone. The maturity that comes with managing anger appropriately must be learned, through much time and practice.

8

From Parent Control to Self-Control

I'm sorry, but you may not go to the party!

As a child moves into the teenage years, discipline and training need to gradually change from a parent-control basis to a parent-trust basis, in which privileges and freedom depend on trustworthiness. When a child is young and has little judgment on how to act, the parents take almost all the responsibility in determining how he should behave. As the child becomes a preadolescent and experiences the drive of independence, he will attempt to exert more and more control and decision-making regarding his own behavior. Parents should work to make this transition as smooth and nontraumatic as possible.

In order to accomplish this, you must first accept the fact that this drive for independence is normal. Eventually your child should become quite independent of you, whether you like it or not. What you want to be able to do is to control the rate of this gain of independence, gauging it on his rate of maturity. The best indicator you have in doing this is the degree to which you can trust your child and his ability to control his behavior.

Your teen will likely test your limits of control as well as your love for him. So, naturally, your great concern is where to set the limits. Should you make them fair, broad, and reasonable? Or should you be very strict? It is important to remember that the normal teenager will test—and sometimes even break—your limits or rules, regardless of where you place them. If you make the rules extremely restrictive, your teenager will always test them, and usually break them. If you make them broad, your teenager will again find some way to challenge them or break them. Common sense, then, indicates that since it is in the makeup of most teenagers to challenge and/or break rules, no matter how strict or broad they are, the sensible thing is to make rules *initially* quite strict and restrictive. Then, as the maturing child demonstrates that he can be trusted to behave appropriately, you can gradually allow him increased privileges with less and less parental control. In other words, his privileges will be contingent upon his showing you that he is trustworthy. As your teenager proves more trustworthy, you trust him more. As he demonstrates appropriate behavior, you increase his privileges. But in order to do this, you must begin from a restrictive position.

There are many advantages to using this approach. First, it is wise to be in the position of being able to allow more privileges and not fewer. Your relationship with your teenager is better when you are able to be positive; it is less comfortable when you must be negative. When your teen is just beginning his adolescent career, especially his social life, if you begin by being somewhat overrestrictive, then you can afford to be positive and grant privileges—you can be the "good guy." However, if you begin by being "broadminded, reasonable, understanding," allowing your budding teenager too many privileges and too few restrictions, you have only one way to go—toward increased restrictiveness or being the "bad guy." Also, if your limits are too broad and lenient, and your teenager breaks them, he will be much more apt to bring harm or disgrace on himself and the family.

I can't overemphasize how important it is to set up the rules that allow you to be as positive as possible. Begin in an overrestrictive way so that you may be able to grant more more and more privileges. If you give all the privileges initially, you have nothing to work with. You have no way to reward your teen for taking increased responsibility. And, worse, you have no means to train him to be trustworthy and learn the value of being responsible.

Your goal in moving from restrictiveness to privilege is that your teenager will become a responsible, trustworthy, independent adult by the age of 18.

This is not easy, for it takes courage and determination to make your teenager's privileges strictly dependent upon his ability to control his own behavior. It takes strength to stand against the pressure for unearned concessions, not only from your teenager, but from other teenagers, other parents, and even society.

But let me tell you one crucial fact—all teenagers at some level of consciousness realize they need guidance and control from their parents. They *want* it. I have heard so many teenagers say that their parents do not love them because they are not strict or firm enough. And so many teenagers express their thankfulness and love to parents who showed their care and concern by their guidance and control

Experiencing Consequences

Another factor to consider is that in order for a teenager to continue to develop a normal conscience and learn to behave responsibly as an adult, he must experience *consequences* for his behavior—positive consequences for appropriate, responsible behavior; and negative consequences for inappropriate, irresponsible behavior. These consequences must be consistent and fair, and based on behavior—not on how the parent is feeling at the time. Again, we're back to facing the importance of parental self-control and making decisions based on clear, logical thinking rather than on our impulsive feelings.

How do you accomplish this? Let's look at one of the most difficult issues as an example—dating. When our daughter Carey was 12, she wanted to start dating. By "dating" she meant single dates with a boy. My wife and I felt Carey was too young to date.

I believe that a rule or decision deserves a reason. A teenager is entitled to know why. And parents must be careful to be sure that the reason is practical and not simply moralistic. Of course, there may be moralistic reasons behind the rule, but there must also be a practical reason. Teenagers in early adolescence are in the midst of questioning their parents' rules and values. And these early teens relate much better to practical rules than to moralistic ones. One reason so many teenagers turn against spiritual values is they they are given too many moralistic reasons for rules and/or restrictions. During these rebellious, defiant, possibly hostile periods, parents are wise to give practical reasons for decisions. Once a reason is given, however, you certainly are not required to defend it like a doctoral thesis. Arguing with your teenager over the adequacy or legitimacy of the reason is seldom warranted. As long as the answer is reasonable, stating it simply is generally sufficient. Being willing to argue about it usually invites further disagreement and anger.

Let's get back to our situation with Carey wanting to date at age 12. We told her that she could not date until she was ready—which we estimated to be in about four years. We left plenty of room for error. Remember, it is far better to be able to become less restrictive than to be forced to become more restrictive.

Carey asked, "Why not?" We explained to her that in this world it is extremely important to be able to function well in groups, and that the age when we learn to operate effectually in groups is early adolescence. There are many adults who never learned to function in groups when they were 12-14 years old and who consequently are "social cripples." Then I dramatically exclaimed, "And no daughter of mine is going to be a social cripple!" We told her that when she learned to function well in groups, then we would talk about other social privileges.

This worked for about a year. Then she came to her mother and me and stated she had learned to operate in groups. We told her she had indeed made good progress, but that being able to function in groups was not simply getting along with everyone. It also meant offering a positive, constructive contribution to the group. It was not merely to be influenced by the group, but to have an influence on the group. We pointed out that she was making excellent progress, but that she was not yet a leader—that the other kids had more influence on her than she did on them. I'm happy to say that Carey increased her group leadership abilities and learned to have a warm, wholesome, gentle, but strong influence not only in her church group but in her school and other organizations.

Protecting Your Teenager

Parents of teenagers need to be in good communication with parents of other teenagers—on a first-name basis, if you will, and especially with the parents of the teenagers who are closest to their own teen. It is a priceless asset to be able to share information and concerns with other parents and to work together with them in providing direction and control for the young people.

I can think of many occasions when Carey would be invited to a social event which we knew nothing about. How grateful we were to be able to call different parents who were equally concerned and willing to check the appropriateness of a party.

How can parents know if a certain event is appropriate or not? Parents must not be hesitant about getting on the telephone and asking questions, no matter who is sponsoring the event. I'm sorry to say that many parents today are not only condoning immoral and destructive influences on youth, but are actively encouraging them.

You should not be afraid to call the parent or adult sponsor to find out about planned activities. How else are you going to control and protect your teenage child? And when you do call, listen carefully to the attitude or tone of what that person tells you, since this usually conveys more than the actual words. For example, when the parent or adult sponsor actually sounds pleased and even thankful that you are calling regarding your teenager, that is a good sign. It's a wonderful thing to hear someone say how grateful they are that a parent cares enough about his child to find out what's going on. When I hear that, I thank God that there are still decent, loving, guiding parents in this world.

Unfortunately, however, you may receive a different response. I remember calling a mother who was giving a party to which Carey, then 15, was invited. This mother's response to my inquiry was hostile. She said, "This is a private party. Your daughter is invited and she can come or not. It's up to her, but what I do in my own home is my business!" From this response alone, I knew that her home was no place for any teenager.

But I pressed her for details. I said, "I see. But I'm concerned about my daughter, and I'd really appreciate it if you would fill me in on the details of your get-together." By now the mother was angry, but with persistance I was able to gather that the teenagers would be served wine and Bloody Marys in a sensually provocative atmosphere.

This is commonplace today. You can't sit back and assume your teenagers are experiencing wholesome influences simply because the activities may be "supervised." You need to work together with other parents to provide wholesome activities and also be able to keep each other informed of what is going on with your children. No one else will do that for you. So many influences today are not what you would want your teenager to be exposed to.

Appropriateness and Trust

You should keep two things in mind as you control and train your teenager. First, allow privileges based upon the trust relationship. Secondly, try to make sure your teenager can handle the particular situation, before you allow him to go.

While these may seem to be conflicting statements, they are not. Too many parents become confused at this point. They may use the trust relationship in deciding on a privilege but fail to check into the circumstances and suitability of the occasion. Checking into the appropriateness of the situation does *not* mean you do not trust your teenager. Even though a teenager is trustworthy, means well, and has fine intentions, there are still situations he may not have the maturity to handle. In these cases, you must protect your teenager.

A good example of this is the party to which Carey was invited. Carey was quite trustworthy—it was her genuine intention to act appropriately. But she was too young and immature at that time to handle such a heavy situation.

When I told Carey she could not go to this event, her natural reaction was, "Why not?" She carefully pointed out that her previous behavior had been exemplary, that she knew how to behave appropriately, that she definitely would do so, and that I could trust her. My reply to her was that she was absolutely right. I was truly proud of her and knew that I could trust her. However, I felt she was not yet ready or able to handle such a pressurized and difficult situation as this particular event. I pointed out that, although my own behavior had also been exemplary and I was trustworthy, I was also a normal person who likewise could be tempted. I could probably handle most any social situation. One evidence of this, which I was able to point out to Carey, was during my navy days when I was required to supervise my division of sailors during their "happy hours" in strip tease and topless bars. But even there, I had certain external restraints on me—such as being in a naval officer's uniform and being completely responsible for the welfare of my men.

Even with these difficult tests of character behind me, I, as well as anyone else, can be tempted beyond my endurance if I am not careful to control my life. So, why should I take the chance of ruining my integrity, character, marriage, spiritual fellowship, welfare of my children, and my life? I pointed out to Carey that this is one reason why I don't go to bars and discos. I trust myself but I have no absolute guarantees that I can manage any temptation. I told her of a well-known minister who felt his calling was among patronizers of bars. I was not surprised to learn of his change of lifestyle which made a mockery of his ministry and his marriage.

I was able to tell Carey that I truly trusted her because of her previous good behavior, but that there were certain situations she was not yet ready to handle—and some that any right-thinking person should avoid.

Delaying

Let's say you give your teenagers privileges based on your trust relationship with them, and also on the appropriateness of each situation. These criteria are spelled out to them so they know why you are making your decisions and that you are trying not to be simply arbitrary. Yet this is not quite the whole picture. For frequently, these types of decisions will be difficult to make.

I remember once when Carey was 15 years old that she was invited to spend the day on a large boat, to swim during the day. Then at night there would be a party aboard the boat. My wife and I were having some tough thoughts about this one. The day activities certainly seemed all right. But the thought of the party that night somehow bothered us. We knew the parents who would supervise the party were sensible people.

At this point, let me insert some good advice: if you ever get into a situation where you do not feel comfortable about an upcoming event that your teenager wants to go to—yet you can't put your finger on the reason why—your best response is *to delay*.

I usually say something like, "Wow, that's a tough one, Honey; let me think it over." In the teenage world, events and situations change so fast that this type of problem usually takes care of itself. I can think of only one or two occasions when the problem did not somehow resolve itself. Another advantage of delay is that your teenager will have time to think it over and may come to some mature decisions himself. In the example of Carey being invited to the day and night party aboard the boat, I said, "Let me think it over." And Carey said, "OK, but hurry; I have to know by Thursday."

Much to my chagrin, the situation had not resolved itself. The questionable event was still on, the weather forecast was excellent, and it was Thursday evening already, with Carey saying in an irritated voice, "What's your answer, Daddy? Greg has to know tonight."

I had a terrible feeling in the pit of my stomach, because I couldn't think of any legitimate reason to say no. Carey's behavior had been exemplary. Just as I was ready to give her permission to go, she said, "Daddy, by the way." (Remember those critical words?) "Greg can't get his folks' car to go to the party; we have to go in his dune buggy—you know, the one with no seat belts—and we have to cross the bridge during the 5 o'clock traffic."

I am surely glad I was listening closely at that moment, for I immediately responded, "I'm sorry, but you may not go to the party."

Carey did not even ask why, but went directly to the phone, called Greg and said, "I'm sorry, I can't go to the party. My father won't let me."

Many times a teenager will give clues when he wants or needs a "No" to a question or privilege. You must listen closely for these clues, for they usually occur when your teenager needs a way out of a difficult peer situation. When he can use you as a defense or alibi in such a situation, this produces a wonderful sense of comraderie between you and your teenager. You should permit your teenager to use you in this way. Of course, you must also be careful not to lie or allow your teen to be dishonest in accomplishing it.

As you can see in Carey's situation, she somehow sensed that she could not handle the boat party at that time and needed a way out. Perhaps it was her discomfort about it that made me uncomfortable. I really don't know. But at any rate I am so thankful Carey took advantage of our parental authority and removed herself from a possibly unwholesome situation.

Looking Ahead

There is another strategy I have found to be invaluable in dealing with the teenager's drive for independence and pressing for more freedom and privileges. The attitude of the parents toward their child's growth to responsible independence will strongly affect a teenager's response to control and authority.

If you approach your teenager with an attitude of keeping him dependent on you, perhaps out of fear, and attempting to actually stifle his growth to independence, he will react poorly. If your teenager yields to this type of attitude, he will be hampered in progressing to responsible adulthood and may become a passive, dependent person. If he resists this overprotective attitude, his relationship with you will, of course, deteriorate and much conflict will result.

So what should your attitude and philosophy be? The most healthy attitude is to work hand in hand with your teenager *toward his being* a responsible, *independent* person by the time he is at the legal age of adulthood. If you clearly state this to your teenager so he understands that you actually *want* him to be independent within a given time and are working toward that end, he can then feel you are for him and not against him.

A teenager needs to be reminded of this partnership from time to time, especially when he wants to go some place which his parents feel is inappropriate. For example, let's say that your teenager wants to go to a party which you have checked out and feel is inappropriate for him. We'll assume you have done a good job in being available and in keeping your teenager's emotional tank full. Also, you have been using the trust relationship effectively in determining what privileges should be given. And you have employed the delay technique, but the problem has not resolved itself. You find that you must now say no. And you find that your teenager simply will not or cannot accept it.

This is a good time to use the strategy I mentioned. I have found it to be very effective in helping the teenager to gain perspective, to understand that his parents are working on his behalf and not trying to hold him back from gaining his independence. In my experience, this difficult time seems to occur most frequently when a teenager is 16. He has recently gotten his driver's license which feeds his urge for new experiences. How forceful you need to be with this strategy depends, of course, on the specific situation.

I remember counseling parents of a 16-year-old boy who was utterly determined to go to a concert which was obviously unwholesome. Up to that time the parents had been able to control his behavior and social development fairly well by using the trust relationship and delay techniques. But this occasion was different. The parents had almost come to the point of letting him go. Of course, this would have been a mistake. We must remember that a teenager needs his parents to be in control at all times. It's all right for parents to change their minds for good reason, but not as capitulation to the teenager's demands.

I advised these fine parents to be pleasant but firm at this time, as they explained to their teenager that they wanted him to become independent and to be able to make his own decisions as soon as he was able. That he was 16½ years old, and they had only 18 months (be sure to put in months to make it seem sooner) to make Randy a completely independent person. In only 18 months he would legally be an adult and after that date, he could be (notice: say *"could be,"* not *"would be"*—don't get yourself in a corner) expected to handle his own affairs, make his own living, find his own place to live, do his own laundry, cooking, etc.

If these facts still do not give your teenager perspective (they do in the majority of cases), and he remains oppositional, you may go furtuer and state that you have no legal responsibility for him after he is 18—that you intend to do everything in your parental power to get him ready for adult life in the next 18 months because your legal responsibility ends at that time. Again, be sure to say *"legal"* to avoid regretting your words later because, of course, parents have other responsibilities to their child after he is 18.

This strategy is a rather harsh thing to do to teenagers, and should only be used as a last resort in difficult circumstances. However, teenagers need to be aware that the parents' overall intention is to indeed prepare them for responsible independence and adulthood, not to hold them back.

You can reinforce this attitude in several ways. For example, providing your teenager with his own checking account, placing monthly deposits into it, and teaching him to be responsible for certain expenses is an excellent way to foster an attitude of cooperation between you and your teen, in working toward his independence. Initially, he should be responsible for buying only a few items. As he learns to assume more responsibility, he can be given additional items to be responsible for, on a graduated scale, with the idea of becoming able by the age of 18, to assume total financial responsibility.

Another way to foster this attitude of working together in gaining independence in your teenager is, during times of good communication, to talk about his future, what he wants to do after high school, what vocation he might consider, whether college is right for him, and if so, which one. Looking at colleges with your teenager is a very effective means of fostering a feeling of cooperation. Providing any new experience for your teenager, such as a new sport or hobby, also helps accomplish this.

Setting Limits

A question frequently raised by parents is how much restriction to impose on a teenager for misconduct. Teenagers, like all children, have an acute sense of fairness. They know when parents are permissive and when they are too harsh or unreasonable. I've seen parents on both ends of the spectrum. Some have extreme difficulty in consistently setting firm limits and are easily manipulated by their teenagers. Other parents take the opposite tack and impose harsh treatment. I know of one teenager who was restricted to her home for over a year for going to a bar. Parents need to remember that the punishment should fit the crime. Common sense must prevail! Lesser misbehavior, such as coming in 15 minutes late after a date, warrants restrictions of less than a week. If it recurs, then the restriction must be lengthened. Restrictions longer than two weeks are seldom warranted, with four weeks as an extreme outside limit. If restrictions are frequent, especially in ranges greater than one week, something is wrong—

possibly in the parents' expectation, the parent-child relationship, or other possibilities which we will discuss later.

Above all, remember that well-loved teenagers are so much easier to discipline and control than those who are not so loved. We must keep their emotional tanks full.

Parent Courtesy

Another point to be aware of is the great importance of parents being considerate and pleasant to their teenagers' peers. They should be cordial, regardless of their feelings toward them. Many needless problems arise as a direct result of parental hostility toward adolescent peers. Remember, parents are authority figures. Most teenagers will consequently pity and side with a peer who is being ill-treated by a parent, regardless of the situation.

One of the most tragic examples of this occurred in the Dempsey family. Jane dated a boy who upset her parents. He was much older than Jane, and was known to deal in drugs. He was also surly and disrespectful toward authority.

Due to several factors, one of the greatest being her parents' extremely hostile way of relating to the boy, Jane became more and more involved with him. Of course, this brought heartache to the parents.

Being civil to anyone, including your teenager's peers, definitely pays off. First of all, your teenager will appreciate it and can feel free to bring other teenagers home. Secondly, other teens often are having problems communicating with their parents. Many times they are seeking other adults to relate to. It is a wonderful privilege to befriend your teenager's friends. Not only does this help them, but it draws your own teen closer to you.

Thirdly, when you treat "unwholesome" peers kindly, you avoid pushing your teenager toward them, as the Dempseys did.

In fact, what usually happens in such a case, is that your teenager will later approach you with questions regarding his peers. He will want your opinion about his friends. Then your teenager will listen to your opinions of his peers. But if you are hostile toward his friends, your teenager usually will avoid discussing that issue with you, and you in turn will have lessened your influence on your child.

Abnormal Situations

What we have talked about thus far bears upon normal situations. However, there are times when parents are not facing normal problems. If a teenager, despite unconditional love and appeals to reason from parents, is continually difficult to manage, it is likely that he has more serious problems and needs outside help.

There are several teenage behavior problems with which parents may be unable to deal. One of these is depression, which can be complex and treacherous on the teenage level. Another problem we are encountering more and more frequently is thought disorders, or difficulty in controlling one's thinking. Still another problem that calls for professional help is neurological disorders with resultant emotional difficulties.

A physician needs to be aware of possible character disorders. One evidence of this is a teenager's inability to handle anger appropriately. Also, a teenager's behavior may be difficult to control because of problems in the family dynamics or relationships. In fact, a teenager's behavioral problems may be caused or aggravated by any combination of these factors. Since behavioral problems in teenagers are becoming more and more common and increasingly complex, a wise parent will seek help early before they become serious. Most problems can be handled effectually by competent, well-trained therapists, along with cooperation from the parents.

9

Adolescent Depression

... I wonder if it would be better to be dead?

Adolescent depression is a complex, subtle, and dangerous phenomenon. It is complex because of its many complicated causes and effects. It is subtle because it almost always goes undetected, even by the teenager, until a tragedy occurs. It is dangerous because depression can result in the worst of happenings—from school failure to suicide.

I see many teenagers who have attempted to harm or kill themselves. Many times their parents and friends are stunned and shocked in disbelief at the action. These distressed people believed that everything was well with their teenagers, never guessing that they were so unhappy.

Teenage depression is difficult to identify because its symptoms are different from the classical symptoms of adult depression. For example, a teenager in mild depression acts and talks normally. There are no outward signs of depression. Mild teenage depression is manifested in fantasies, in daydreams, or in dreams during sleep. Mild depression is detectable only by somehow knowing the child's thought pattern and thought content. Few professionals even can pick up depression in this state.

In moderate depression, also, the teenager acts and talks

normally. However, in moderate depression, the content of the teenager's speech is affected, dwelling primarily on depressing subjects such as death, morbid problems, and crises. Since many adults today seem to dwell on pessimistic trains of thought, the teenager's depression may go unnoticed.

A short time ago, an anxious mother called me regarding her 14-year-old son. She was not sure if her son needed help. This loving mother said her boy was acting normally, looked normal, and talked normally—that everything seemed fine—except that every evening after watching the news, he would say something like this: "Things are getting so bad in the world, I wonder if it would be better to be dead." This fine boy was found to be moderately depressed.

Moderate depression in adults, on the other hand, can be quite crippling. It can cause severe sleeping and eating problems, and inability to function in various capacities, from parenting to vocation. It may lead to serious consequences, even suicide.

Moderate depression in teenagers is just as profound and serious as moderate depression in adults. Biochemically and neurohormonally, the two are essentially identical. But you see how different the manifestations or symptoms are. A moderately depressed adult looks terrible, feels miserable, and is severely affected in his ability to function. But the teenager? In the vast majority of cases, only in severe depression does the teenager actually appear depressed. When we can say, "Boy, does that kid look depressed!" we should assume that that teenager is profoundly depressed and probably suicidal.

There is an exception to this, however. Teenage depression is difficult to identify because teens are good at "masking" it; that is, they can cover it by appearing OK even when they are absolutely miserable. This is often called *smiling depression*. This is a front which teenagers employ unconsciously. This masking of depression is done primarily when other people are around. When depressed teenagers are alone, they let down or relax the mask somewhat.

This is helpful to parents. If we are able to see our teenagers at times when they believe no one is looking at them, we may be able to identify depression. It is an amazing thing to see the transformation in the face. Alone they will appear terribly sad and miserable. As soon as they think someone is watching, the smiling mask of depression immediately appears as though nothing is wrong. This is one way of identifying depression, although it is not the best way.

Discovering Depression

How, then, can we discover depression in our teenagers so that we can do something about it before tragedy occurs? It is imperative that we be able to identify it early, since there are numerous ways today in which depression can bring harm to our children. A depressed teenager is quite susceptible to unhealthy peer pressure, is prone to fall victim to drugs, alcohol, criminal activity, inappropriate sexual experiences, and other antisocial behaviors, including suicide.

The best way to identify depression in a teenager is to understand the various symptoms manifested in teenage depression and how they develop. It is crucial to understand the total constellation of symptoms in detail, because one or two symptoms may or may not signify true depression. True depression is a biochemical and neurohormonal process that in teenagers usually develops slowly over a period of weeks or months.

Before we study the specific symptoms of adolescent depression, we should understand that a depressed adolescent may also have one or more of the classic symptoms of adult depression, including feelings of helplessness, hopelessness, despondency, and despair; problems with sleep (either too much or too little); problems with eating (too much or too little with weight loss); lack of energy; feelings of low self-worth; problems handling anger.

Now let's look at the more specific symptoms of adolescent depression:

1. *Shortened attention span.* In mild teenage depression, the first symptom generally seen is a shortening of attention span. The teenager is not able to keep his mind focused on a subject as long

as he once could. His mind drifts from what he wants to focus on and he becomes increasingly distractable. He finds himself daydreaming more and more. This shortening of attention span usually becomes obvious when the teen attempts to do his homework. He finds it harder and harder to keep his mind on it. And it seems that the harder he tries, the less he accomplishes. Of course, this leads to frustration, as the teenager then blames himself for being "stupid" or "dumb." He assumes that he does not have the intellectual ability to do the work. Imagine what this does to his self-esteem.

2. *Daydreaming.* The shortened attention span affects the teenager in the classroom. At first, he may be able to pay attention to the classwork for most of the period, and then daydream the remaining minutes. As the depression deepens and the attention span becomes shorter, the teenager pays attention less, and daydreams more. At this point, his teacher is in the best position to identify depression. Unfortunately, daydreaming is usually interpreted as laziness or poor attitude. However, just one or two symptoms alone, such as daydreaming and short attention span, do not allow a person to make the diagnosis of true adolescent depression. We must see a gradual development of a constellation of symptoms.

3. *Poor grades.* As the teenager's attention span shortens, and his daydreaming increases, the natural result is lower grades. Unfortunately, this falling of grades is usually so gradual that it is difficult to notice. For this reason, it is seldom associated with depression. In fact, the teenager, the parents, and the teacher usually assume that the work is too difficult for the teenager or that he is becoming more interested in other things. It would be quite helpful if the grades took a drastic plunge, an A to D in one grading period. This would arouse the appropriate concern. However, the grades usually go something like this: A, A-, B+, B. Depression is seldom considered.

4. *Boredom.* As the teenager daydreams more and more, he gradually falls into a state of boredom. Boredom is normal in teenagers, especially in early adolescence, but only for relatively

short periods of time. Normal boredom is frequently seen for an hour or two, sometimes for an entire evening or day, or occasionally even two days. But prolonged boredom, several days or more, is not normal, and should be a warning to us that something is not right. Few things worry me as much as prolonged boredom in an adolescent, especially in an early adolescent. Boredom usually manifests itself in the teenager wanting to stay by himself in his own room for increasingly longer periods of time. He spends this time just lying on the bed, daydreaming and listening to music. The bored teenager loses interest in things which he or she once enjoyed, for example, sports, clothes, cars, hobbies, clubs, church and social activities, and dating.

5. *Somatic depression.* As the boredom continues and deepens, the teenager gradually slips into moderate depression. At this point, he begins to suffer from what I call *somatic depression.* I use this term because, even though all depression is physiological, or has a biochemical-neurohormonal basis, at this point, the symptoms begin to affect the child in a directly physical way. For example, in moderate depression, the teenager begins to experience physical pain. This pain may occur in many places, but is most often felt in the lower midchest region or as headaches. Many teenagers suffer pain in the lower chest and/or head, secondary to depression.

6. *Withdrawal.* In this miserable state the teenager may withdraw from peers. And to make matters worse, he doesn't simply avoid his peers, but may disengage himself from them with such hostility, belligerence, and unpleasantness that he alienates them. As a result, the teenager becomes very lonely. And since he has so thoroughly antagonized his good friends, he finds himself associating with rather unwholesome peers who may use drugs and/or are frequently in trouble. The situation becomes more frightening.

Once prolonged boredom has set in, many things can develop. The mental and physical pain at this stage may be excruciating and at times unbearable. A teenager in this state cannot tolerate his misery indefinitely. Eventually, he becomes desperate enough to do something about his misery. Most amazingly, even at this point the teenager is hardly ever aware that he is depressed. The teenager's ability to hide behind denial is truly incredible. This is why depression is seldom suspected until tragedy occurs.

Acting Out Depression

When a teenager has been moderately to severely depressed to the extent that he can endure it no longer, he will take action in an attempt to alleviate his misery and distress. The teenager's action resulting from depression is termed "acting out his depression." There are many ways for a teenager to act out his depression.

Boys tend to be more violent than girls. They may attempt to relieve their depressive symptoms by stealing, lying, fighting, driving fast, or through other types of antisocial behavior. One of the most common kinds of criminal behavior seen today among boys is *breaking and entering*. Doing something which has an air of excitement and danger to it seems to somewhat relieve the pain of depression. Breaking into homes provides this air, and is therefore commonly resorted to by depressed boys.

Of course, there are also other reasons boys break into homes. Therefore, when a teenager is referred to me for behavior such as breaking and entering, one of my first concerns is to find how much depression has played into the teenager's behavior. This is critical because a depressed teenager generally does not respond well to help if the depression is not treated also. I believe that overlooking the depression in these young people is totally negligent. And unfortunately, most agencies dealing with teens focus on behavior and are unaware of the depressive component in the child's problem.

Girls tend to act out their depression in less violent ways. However, because of unhealthy, violence-oriented models in the media, this trend is changing. Girls frequently act out their depression by *sexual promiscuity*. Their depressive pain tends to be allieviated during the close physical relationship of intercourse. However, when the act is over, these unfortunate girls feel worse—more depressed—than before, because of the self-degradation involved. Depression and low self-esteem are almost always the basis of a girl's promiscuity. It is amazing how much we can help a girl with this type of problem, by taking care of her depression. It is equally true how little we can do if we neglect her depression.

A depressed teenager can also act out his depression by taking *drugs*. Marijuana and depression are a very dangerous combination because marijuana actually makes a depressed teenager feel better. Marijuana is not an antidepressant. Rather, it blocks the pain of depression. Unfortunately, the teenager feels better simply because he does not hurt as much. Of course, when the marijuana is out of his system, the depressive pain returns. Then in order to obtain the same degree of relief from the pain, the teenager must use a greater quantity. This is a common way for a teenager to become habituated to marijuana, to become a "pothead." Other drugs can affect a depressed teenager in the same way. So naturally, when we attempt to help a teenager on drugs, we must determine how great a role depression is playing in his drug usage. I am genuinely alarmed how depression is overlooked or discounted by many professionals and agencies involved in treating adolescent drug problems.

Another way a depressed teenager may act out his depression is by attempting *suicide*. Sometimes the attempt is a gesture in which the teenager does not wish death, but attention. At other times, there is a genuine attempt to die. Girls make many more suicide attempts than boys, but boys are more often successful in killing themselves. Girls generally use less violent means of attempting suicide, such as pills. Boys, on the other hand, use more violent means, such as guns. Of course, this makes it easier to save girls from their own attempts. However, I have seen many girls come extremely close to death or actually die. What a tragedy!

Remedy for Mild Depression
What can we do to help our depressed teenagers? First of all, we must identify depression early in order to prevent tragedy. This means we must be familar with symptoms of adolescent depression. People who need this information most are parents and those

who work with teenagers, such as teachers, school counselors, and youth workers. When the depression is identified early, that is, when the depression is mild, it is relatively easy to halt its insidious progress and alleviate it.

Although most adolescent depression is complex in its underlying causes, often there is a specific factor or event which finally overwhelms the child and triggers the constellation of symptoms. For example, a death or illness, or departure of a person important to the teenager, a disappointment such as a divorce or conflict between parents, or a move to an undesired place. In such situations, the teenager feels lonely, abandoned, and unloved. It is crucial, first of all, to show him we do care about him and love him. We show this by spending enough time with him to permit his psychological defenses to come down in order for him to be able to meaningfully communicate with us. Then our love-giving, that is, eye contact, physical contact, and focused attention, will be meaningful to him.

If the problem is a conflict within the family, for example a divorce, the teenager needs help in dealing with his own feelings about this. He especially needs to realize that the divorce is not his fault—that there was nothing he could do to prevent it.

Teenagers are extremely sensitive to problems between their parents. Unfortunately, most people seem to believe that once a teenager finishes high school and leaves home, he is not really affected by what happens between the parents. How utterly wrong this is.

I remember the first time we visited my daughter after she went away to college. We went with about 20 of her friends for a snack one evening. All of Carey's friends were freshmen, away from home for the first time. Every one of them stated how much they loved school, their new friends, and college life, but they also voiced distress that they received so little communication from their parents. Few phone calls, letters, or visits.

Most parents simply do not realize how traumatic this period is in a young person's life, and how important it is to continue to provide a solid, stable "home base." About the worst time for

113

parents to divorce is around the time the teenager leaves home. Going away from home, especially for the first time, is one of the most unsettling, anxiety-provoking, and insecure parts of anyone's life. At that time, a teenager's primary foundation of security is in his parents and home. Divorce at that time utterly shatters these sources of teenage stability. But it is amazing how naive so many people are, and how many parents have divorced right after their child has gone off to college. This has a profound effect on the teenager's value system, undermining his faith in the sanctity of marriage. It leaves him little opportunity to resolve his feeling of frustration, anger, anxiety, rejection, and fear regarding his parents before he himself considers marriage. Some of this unresolved inner conflict may affect his own marriage and cause conflict with his spouse.

Moderate and Severe Depression

As depression deepens within a teenager, a serious complication develops. His thought process begins to be affected. In moderate and severe depression, the teenager gradually loses his ability to think clearly, logically, and rationally. His judgment deteriorates as he loses the ability to maintain healthy perspective, and he focuses more and more on morbid, depressing details. His perceptions of reality become distorted, especially concerning what he perceives other people are thinking about him. He more and more assumes that everything is bleak, nothing is worthwhile, and life is not worth living.

He now has a thought disturbance. As the teenager increasingly loses his ability to think and communicate in a clear rational way, counseling per se becomes less and less effective. This is a frightening predicament. How can you help a teenager in counseling when you cannot reason with him? When this situation occurs, medical help is mandatory. For it is usually when the teenager loses his ability to be rational, reasonable, and logical, that he begins to act out his depression in self-destructive ways.

Adolescent depression is not something you can consider a phase that will run its course. This insidious affliction tends to grow worse and worse unless the depression is identified and intervention is taken.

Depression and Drugs

As we mentioned, a depressed teenager is quite susceptible to drug usage for two reasons. First, many drugs, especially marijuana, block (or dull) the pain of depression. Secondly, many sources today are telling our youth that drugs are all right to use. It is common for some professionals or even agencies to tell teenagers that it is all right to use marijuana as long as they do not drink alcohol. It is amazing how many teenagers and adults actually believe that marijuana is harmless. Every day we see the effect of this subtly hazardous drug.

Recently we admitted a 15-year-old boy to the hospital for drug abuse, severe depression, and behavioral problems. Included in our initial evaluation, of course, were the physician's examinations and blood tests. We found this child to be severely anemic. His body was gradually losing its ability to manufacture blood due to drug abuse. Before we could treat the child for his psychological problems, we had to transfer him to a university medical center for a blood marrow transplant. His prognosis is very poor.

All this leads back to parental control of a teenager's freedom, by allowing privileges and freedoms based on trust and trustworthiness and on the appropriateness of the activity. If your teenager genuinely feels that you love and care about him, he will likely listen to you and heed your advice regarding his safety. Therefore, you must keep his emotional tank full. Then you will be able to help your child avoid harmful consequences of yielding to peer pressure to use drugs. You must continue to remind your teenager not to carelessly drink or eat something, without being sure that no one has slipped a drug into the drink or food. At any questionable party, it is good common sense to avoid open punch bowls or accepting food and drink from someone your teenager does not know well. This may sound overly suspicious, but I have personally seen how a single ingestion of a drug can harm a teen's developing mind.

The most frightening aspect of drugs is the way it affects a teenager's thought process. I have seen numerous teenagers who could not think sequentially or logically even after one dose of drugs. This disturbance of thought process is often so subtle that no one detects it, but the results are devastating. The teenager's ability to relate positively to people deteriorates. He comes up with wrong and often bizarre ideas about people, values, authority, society, and himself. He misinterprets people and their motivations. Worst of all, because he cannot think clearly, he becomes somewhat confused and is easily led by peer groups, cults, and other people interested only in using him.

What is more frightening than people who cannot think accurately and have distorted ideas, distorted views, and distorted values? Are you willing to make sure your teenager gets through adolescence without his intellectual, social, and psychological assets being harmed or destroyed? If so, you will love your teenager, take close care of and appropriately supervise him. It is a difficult job, but the reward is well worth the cost. Seeing your teenager developing into a mature, sensitive, independent, right-thinking adult, contributing to his world, is one of life's greatest rewards.

10

Helping Your Teenager Intellectually

It is very important to teach your teenager to think rationally, logically and sequentially.

To prepare your adolescents for the future in this world of nonreason, you must teach them to think clearly. There are two basic reasons for this. First, a person cannot have a strong, consistent, lasting faith or a moral value system without being able to think clearly. A faith which is solid and enduring and provides the basis for life's meaning cannot be a blind faith. It must be based on rational, logical reason. It must be consistent with the real world. And it must provide reasonable answers to life's deepest questions.

The second reason you must teach your young people to think clearly is that there are so many decisions made and actions taken, which are not based on careful, logical thought but on irrational, impulsive whims.

A good example of this was the 1979 takeover of the American Embassy in Iran. Regardless of how you interpret the causes for the seizure, the act did not make *rational* sense. The only way to understand it was to realize the unreasonable emotional fury behind it. While the Iranian capture of the hostages may seem like an isolated incident, the type of thinking that controlled the entire situation is more common than we like to admit. It is so easy for us to assume that persons who perpetrate or defend unreasonable actions really *do* understand the facts, and are simply using fanatical means to obtain their demands. How I wish that were the case! For then they could be reasoned with. *The fact is that this type of person truly believes he is acting rationally and logically.*

It is very important that you teach your teenager to think rationally, logically, and sequentially (keeping facts in proper order). One of the best pieces of armament you can give your child is the ability to evaluate his own thinking so that he can have confidence in it, and be able to modify it in light of new knowledge. In addition, he should learn to see errors in faulty thinking, and understand how false conclusions are reached. How do you help your teenager do this?

Intellectual Development

It is important to understand that a child develops intellectually from one phase to another. The factor which most determines how well a child masters each stage of thought development is the degree of emotional nourishment he receives. The better job you do in unconditionally and genuinely loving your child, the better able he will be to develop intellectually. The more your child feels loved, the more he will be able to learn to think clearly and logically. The less a child feels loved and cared for, the weaker his mind may be.

For his mind to grow in a strong, healthy manner, the teenager must first feel good about himself. Then he will be able to mature into a wise and understanding person who can maintain proper perspective, especially over his emotions. The young person who is not well nourished emotionally may have poor thought control and be overcome and overcontrolled by his feelings. You must meet your teenager's emotional needs first.

Recently, I saw a muscularly built 14-year-old boy, who had attacked his baseball coach with a bat and injured him. The boy felt totally justified in his act. He stated that he had the right to attack his coach because he and the coach's son were competing for the same position, and this put him at a disadvantage.

The poor reasoning that this boy expressed is called *loose association*. By using loose association in the thought process, a person can justify almost anything. Such confused thinking is illogical and dangerous. And it is becoming more and more common among our teenagers today. Unfortunately, this faulty thought process is subtle, and difficult to identify in casual relationships. But it is one of the primary reasons many of our teens are not being prepared for mature adult life.

You should be constantly alert for opportunities to teach your teenager to make correct, accurate associations in his thinking. A typical adolescent cannot think abstractly to a significant degree until he is at least 15 years old, and then he is just learning. This is why a teenager is often sure his parents are wrong or ignorant, during his early and middle adolescence; later, as his thought process matures and he becomes capable of abstract reasoning, he begins to understand his parents and respect their opinions.

You need to be patient and loving during these difficult times and gently train your teenager to think clearly. And one way to do this is to identify faulty association of ideas and correct it.

Intellectual Affirmation

A teenager needs intellectual affirmation to learn to think well. To be able to think creatively, a person must respect himself, not only emotionally and physically but also intellectually. He must feel approval regarding his ability to think. This does not mean giving the impression that you believe he is always right. It is rather encouraging him in a growing self-respect for his ability to reason and solve problems.

Most teenagers cannot feel this self-assurance and self-approval without first receiving assurance and approval from their parents or parent figures. Many parents make the mistake of only correcting their teenagers. But a teen will feel competent only if he receives approval, validation, and praise, as well as correction.

You can give these priceless assets to your teenagers only if you engage them intellectually. This means being available to discuss with them any subject they want to talk about. It means being willing to listen to their ideas and to fully hear them out, regardless of your own reaction. Then, instead of directly pointing out their mistakes or arguing with them, you can discuss the issues, with respect, seriously considering their viewpoint, and calmly expressing your own. Such conversation should resemble talk between good friends. In doing this, you are not giving up your parental authority. You are simply showing respect for your teenagers' thinking. You are letting them know that their thoughts and opinions are worthy and valuable. If your teens feel that you love and respect them, they will gradually incorporate some of your opinions and values into their thinking.

Unfortunately, too many parents refuse to talk with their teenagers in a give-and-take manner. Instead, they persist in talking down to their teenagers as though they were small children. This makes teens feel that their opinions don't matter. They are not being intellectually affirmed. They are not feeling genuinely loved by their parents. They do not feel respected, and they become hurt and angry.

Add to this the fact that they have not learned whether their thinking is correct or incorrect, logical or irrational. They have had no feedback from parents about whether their ideas are meaningful.

Most teenagers do not know if they are right or wrong about the subjects they think about. This pushes them toward taking the opinions of others, who may not have their welfare at heart. When they become too alienated from family to accept the opinions and values of parents and other legitimate authority figures, they begin listening to people who desire to harm them mentally, emotionally, physically, or spiritually.

You want to make sure your teenager feels unconditionally loved, through use of eye contact, physical contact, and focused attention. Give him intellectual affirmation by listening to him, and carefully noticing the way he thinks and comes to conclusions. Respect him by giving your opinion, without criticizing him or denouncing his thinking.

Only when your teenager sees that you are willing to relate to him as a responsible person with a mind of his own will he feel a balanced confidence in his ability to learn to think clearly and grow to intellectual maturity.

When you criticize your teen's opinions, he will probably feel angry, resentful, and even bitter. And he may become more defiant and resistant to change. If this happens he will hold to immature, selfish, and incorrect opinions, and carry these with him into his adult life. We all know adults who believe incorrect and strange ideas. These unfortunate people have difficulty understanding social, spiritual, or emotional relationships. They tend to jump on the current bandwagon, and often hold unrealistic and antagonistic opinions.

Teach by Example

As a parent, I have made my share of mistakes. So it certainly has its advantages to be the writer of this book, because I can choose the illustrations I wish to share. Let me give you one example that involves the intellectual training of our son, David. I think I handled this situation correctly, as I attempted without criticizing him to show him where his thinking was illogical and too simplistic, and then to teach him more mature ways of thinking.

David knows which TV programs his mother and I approve of and which ones we don't. And he is usually quite good in complying with our wishes regarding his TV viewing. One evening, however he was watching a program we don't like— "Love Boat." When I reminded David that I did not want him to watch it, he asked, "Why not?" and then said he could see nothing wrong with it because "no one is hurting anyone."

Does this reasoning sound familiar? David's statement exemplifies the current state of morality in our society: "I can do what I want as long as it doesn't hurt anyone else." But this attitude is the very thing Pat and I object to in some TV programs, for there is a subtle and dangerous philosophy that underlies the words.

It was very tempting for me to jump on David and criticize him for this shallow and immature way of thinking. But, thank goodness, I remembered that he needs *intellectual affirmation* and *training* to learn to think maturely.

So I said, "I understand what you mean, David, but I think 'Love Boat' is hedonistic and narcissistic." (That got his attention.)

He replied, "What does that mean?"

I said, "Tell you what, David. Let's get a dictionary and look these words up." (Incidentally, using the dictionary has been a tremendous help to me in teaching my children difficult concepts.)

We looked the words up *together*. Then we talked about the meaning of *hedonistic* and *narcissistic* until I was sure he understood them. But, like a typical, developing, early adolescent, after David understood the definitions, he still did not understand how they related to real life. I said, "David, do you think a hedonistic and narcissistic person could make a good husband, wife, mother, or father? How about your mother? Is she selfish? Does she care only about herself with little regard for others? Is she only concerned about her own pleasure and not in anyone else's welfare?" This certainly turned on a light in David's head. He thought about all the things his loving mother had done for him that day, even though she did not feel well.

I was overjoyed when David finally replied, "This means that a selfish person is interested only in getting pleasure for himself, instead of caring about other people."

Then David and I talked about how "Love Boat" displayed selfish, self-gratifying attitudes, with little regard for the welfare of the other person.

Teaching a teenager to think clearly is difficult, time-consuming, and tedious. But if you do not clarify issues, such as those just described, those attitudes will subtly influence your teenager.

Be Consistent

One reason teenagers are confused about moral issues is that many parents are not assuming responsibility for teaching their own convictions to their children. Other parents say they believe in spiritual values but they do not live them. Many parents—including Christians—are having difficulty with their own behavior. The rise in sexual misconduct, child abuse, and cheating is alarming.

Nothing is more confusing to a teenager than inconsistency in the life of the parent. Especially about matters that the parents say they highly value and then treat as less than nothing. How can parents teach their teenagers to think clearly about moral and spiritual values, if their own lives do not demonstrate the results of clear thinking?

I believe that the undisciplined behavior which is destroying the moral fiber of our society must be dealt with. Surely God will judge us for the lack of discipline and self-control in the lives of so many who call themselves Christians.

Fellow parents, let's get our own lives in order, consistently behaving as we know God wants us to. Then we can claim God's promises to us for our children.

11

Helping Your Teenager Spiritually

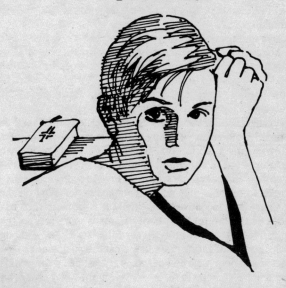

Why are so many of our adolescents apathetic?

Today's generation of teenagers is often called the "apathetic generation." Unfortunately, many of our teenagers are apathetic, especially regarding the future. Many of these young people who are the future hope of our country and way of life lack the vitality, vivaciousness, and eagerness which we love to see.

Why are so many of our adolescents apathetic? Why do they lack initiative and incentive? Essentially it is because they have little hope in the future. Such hopelessness is more serious than the aggressive and violent protestings of the late 1960s. Although the young people of those years had a cause which was at times misdirected and poorly carried out, they at least had a cause which reflected a hope—a hope in their country, in their way of life, and most importantly in themselves.

We do not see this today. The prevailing mood in our young today is *hopelessness, helplessness,* and *despair.* As parents, we wonder how this heartbreaking situation can be possible. It seems as if the very heart and soul have been torn from so many of our precious teenagers. Why do they have so little hope in the future?

It is easy to point out the disheartening world and national developments like genocide in Cambodia, world hunger, Russian aggression, pollution, etc. But these are *not* the cause of teenage hopelessness and despair.

Our forefathers faced equally difficult, dangerous, and frustrating times in the past and with even less security. They faced such hardships as the Great Depression, the holocaust, and other horrors of World War II. But the young people of those eras did not feel the hopelessness and despair seen today.

The attitudes and moods of a nation's youth reflect the attitudes and moods of its adults. Sometimes the youth rally behind their elders, especially when national security is threatened. At other times the young people march against the status quo, especially when they perceive hypocrisy. But today we see neither pro nor con, but rather a foreboding inertia. What are our youth reflecting from adults? They are reflecting depression, gloom, hopelessness, and despair. How can a teenager react positively in such an atmosphere? A teen needs to see something positive and worthwhile in life to rally behind.

Unfortunately, teenagers have little historical perspective to allow them to look back and learn from the experiences of their forebearers. They are limited to the present and future. Therefore, they form their attitudes and moods from the *current, prevailing climate of the present,* and the *current, prevailing attitudes about the future.*

One of the main reasons our teenagers are having problems in forming positive attitudes is that we adults are not passing on to them that determination, hope, and encouragement necessary for facing the future. We of the older generation seem to be offering our young people some strange and unhealthy attitudes which are largely untrue and certainly not scriptural. Almost without realizing it, we adults are rapidly developing an orientation to life which is unwholesome, noncreative, retreating, and passive. We have let other people determine our value system and outlook on life. Many of us believe:

- that we are the first generation to face crises;
- that the world was somehow a nicer, better, and safer place to live before the present problems developed;

127

• that the world is deteriorating so rapidly that it is hopeless and foolish to plan or prepare for the future, since there may not be a future at all. You could rightly expect a teenager, who knows little about the history of man and less about the great promises of God, to succumb to this suffocating, hope-robbing pessimism.

We have become a people whose attitudes and value systems are so easily influenced by others. We tend to feel despair when something is not as good as it once was, ignoring the things which *are* good. We forget to count our blessings. I have seen people despair over the most inconsequential things. On the other hand, we tend to overreact positively to equally unimportant things, like a new car or new clothes. Why should we think it strange that our young are so easily influenced by rock groups and cults when we are equally influenced by television and special interest groups?

I can understand a nonbeliever feeling this disorientation, confusion, and despair. But I find it difficult to understand the Christian person being in this trap of hopelessness. And yet I see so many Christians yielding to pessimistic influences. And I see their teenagers failing to find that critical, peace-giving anchor of hope which Christ intends for His people.

I would like our teenagers to receive messages of *hope*, *encouragement*, and *challenge*. But our generation has generally lost contact with its *spiritual heritage*. Yes, we have problems, some of which are totally new—but so did many of our grandfathers and grandmothers. Why can't we face our crises and difficulties without foreboding, depression, without feelings of hopelessness and doom?

Doomsday?

In times of trouble some religious groups and teachers have tried to escape responsibility by withdrawing and waiting for doomsday. Instead of using biblical passages as God intended—as words of hope and promise—these self-proclaimed prophets use these Scriptures to pronounce an imminent doomsday. Their message is one of hopelessness: The end is coming soon, so there is no point in solving our problems, or providing a better life for our children.

This results in a state of spiritual and emotional paralysis. It also encourages the attitude, "Eat, drink, and be merry, for tomorrow we die."

Imagine being an adolescent in such an atmosphere. At the time when he should be preparing himself for a life of accomplishment to contribute to his world, he senses that the general attitude is to make the best of today, because tomorrow, even if it comes, may not be worth living.

Such preoccupations are breaking the back of responsibility in both adolescents and adults. After reading a book on the "end times" recently offered on TV, one mother admitted, "I can't help wondering why I should raise my kids or try to prepare them for a nonexistent future." A man who read another doomsday book stated, "I feel like giving up my job and just quitting. Why go on?"

In this atmosphere of escalating eschatological futility, it is difficult for people to fight cynicism, to avoid drugs, or to keep from copping out. When doomsday is proclaimed from every Christian media without the proper balance of hope and trust in God's promises and Christ's love, is it any wonder that Christians are finding it increasingly difficult to live responsible, courageous, and productive lives?

Pessimism is not the teaching of Christ. His message is one of hope and joy. Speaking of the last days, Christ said, "But of that day and that hour knoweth no man, no, not the angels which are in heaven, neither the Son, but the Father. Take ye heed, watch and pray: for ye know not when the time is" (Mark 13:32-33, KJV). We are to watch for His coming and to pray. We are not to give up, or be pessimistic about the future. We are not to withdraw from our moral responsibility to live godly lives and to pass our values on to our children. The Scriptures encourage us to be joyful, optimistic, hopeful, and to assume the best.

Most of us are falling prey to the subtle influences of doomsday prophets and becoming more and more pessimistic and fearful. This is *wrong,* for we are to obey Christ, and He tells us to have *faith* and hope. Faith in Him and His words produce comfort, peace, optimism. Such faith gives guidance and strength to solve our problems and to look to the future with confidence. Our teenagers are reflecting our depression, despair, and pessimism because we have lost perspective of our spiritual heritage.

If we as parents can grasp the total picture of history, we will see our place in it—a place of extreme importance and excitement. We are only one chapter in God's plans and book of history. And His plans and history will never end. When our chapter is over, I for one, want to look back and know that we as His people have carried out His will, that we have stood firm in our faith in Him and in His goodness. I want to feel good about not giving in to the world's pressures to use our resources for "experiences" today at the expense of sacrificing our God-given privilege to live righteous, godly lives. I want to be able to say with Paul, "I have fought a good fight, I have finished my course, I have kept the faith" (2 Timothy 4:7, KJV).

God help us to finish our course and keep the faith. For to do this to the best of our ability will give more to our teenagers than anything else. But to give our teenagers hope, faith, and optimism, we must live it.

"Show Me How to Live"

One of the main cries of adolescents today is for their parents to provide them ethical and moral value systems to guide them. This is expressed by teenagers in various ways. One child states he wants a "standard to live by." Another teenager needs a "meaning in life." Other desperate teens yearn for "something to show me how to live" or "something to hold on to" or "a higher guidance."

These desperate yearnings are not experienced by only a few discontented, unhappy youngsters. Most teenagers are feeling these needs and are confused, so terribly confused, in this all-important area of their lives. Unfortunately, it is quite unusual to find teenagers who sense meaning and purpose in their lives, who are at peace with themselves, and who have a healthy perspective about living in a confusing, rapidly changing, and frightening world.

Initially a child looks to his parents for guidance in life. Whether

130

the child is successful in finding this from his parents depends on two things: whether his parents have found direction for themselves, and whether the child can accept parental values and make them his own. A child who is not able to feel genuinely loved by his parents will find this difficult.

Let's examine the first requirement in providing the meaning to life a young person so desperately needs. We parents need a foundation on which we base our own lives and which can stand the test of time. A foundation which will see us through every part of life, through marital needs, money crises, problems with our children, energy shortages, and clashes within a changing society where spiritual standards are rapidly weakening. We parents must possess that foundation to be able to pass it on to our own children.

This priceless, comfort-providing, peace-giving treasure which every heart needs is a Person. He is extremely personal, yet can be shared with another person. He gives strength in times of stress, yet offers comfort in times of sadness. He grants us wisdom when we are confused, yet corrects us when we are wrong. He provides help when we are needy, and His help will never end. For He guides us continually and stays "closer than a brother."

He gives commands to be carried out, but promises wonderful rewards for obedience. At times He allows loss, distress, and pain, but He always gives us something better. He does not impose Himself upon us, but patiently waits for us to invite Him into our lives. He does not force us to do His will, but is painfully disappointed when we do the wrong thing. He desires that we love Him because He first loved us, but He allows us a free will to choose Him or reject Him. He wants to take care of us, but refuses to force Himself upon us. His greatest desire is to be our Father, but He will not intrude. If we want what He wants—a loving, caring, Father-child relationship with Him—we must accept His offer. He is too considerate to force it. He is waiting for you and me to become His children. Of course, as you have guessed He must be a personal God.

This personal, intimate relationship wit' God through His Son

Jesus Christ is the most important thing in life. This is the "something" which our young people are yearning for: "the meaning in life," "something to count on," "something to bring comfort when everything seems to be falling apart." It is all there.

Do you have it? If you do not, seek help from a minister or a Christian friend.

The second requirement is that a child identify with his parents so that he can accept and incorporate their values.

As you recall, if a teenager does not feel loved and accepted, he has real difficulty identifying with his parents, and tends to react to parental guidance with anger, resentment, and hostility. He views each parental request (or command) as an imposition and learns to resist it. In severe cases, a teenager learns to consider each parental request with such resentment that his total orientation to parental authority (and eventually to all authority, including God's) is to do the opposite of what is expected of him. When this degree of alienation occurs, it is nearly impossible for parents to give their moral and ethical value systems to their teenager.

In order for a teen to identify with his parents, relate closely with them, and be able to accept their standards, he must feel genuinely loved and accepted by them. To lead a teen to the close relationship with God which they possess, parents must make sure that a child feels unconditionally loved. It is extremely difficult for teenagers who do not feel unconditionally loved by their parents to feel loved by God.

Religious Training

A very important thing to know about a teenager is how his memory operates. Remember that a teenager is a child emotionally and is much more emotional than cognitive. He therefore retains feelings much more readily than facts. A child can remember how he felt in a particular situation much easier than he can remember the details of what went on.

Let me give you a very pertinent example. A child or teenager in a Sunday School class will remember exactly how he felt long after he forgets what was said or taught.

So, in some ways, whether a child's experience was pleasant or unpleasant is much more important than the details of what a teacher taught. By *pleasant* I do not mean that a teacher need cater to a child's desire for fun and frolic. I mean that the teacher should treat the child with respect, kindness, and concern, and make him feel good about himself. The child should not be criticized, humiliated, or otherwise put down.

If religious training is a degrading or boring experience for a young person, he is likely to reject even the best teaching, especially if morality and ethics are involved. It is from this type of situation that a teenager develops a bias against religious matters, and tends to consider church people as hypocrites. This attitude is difficult to rectify and can continue with him for a lifetime.

On the other hand, if the learning experience is a pleasant one, a teenager's memories of religious things will be pleasant and can then be incorporated into his personality. Emotionality and spirituality are not entirely separate entities. One is quite related to and dependent upon the other. For this reason, if parents want to help a child spiritually, they must care for him emotionally. Because a child remembers feelings much more easily than facts, there must be a series of pleasant memories within which to accumulate the facts—especially spiritual facts.

The Wait-and-Choose Approach

I would like to examine a popular misconception that goes something like this: "I want my child to learn to make his own decisions after he is exposed to things. He shouldn't feel he has to believe what I believe. I want him to learn about different religions and philosophies; then when he has grown up he can make his own decision."

This parent is either copping out or is grossly ignorant of the world we live in. A child brought up in this manner is to be pitied. Without continual guidance and clarification in ethical, moral, and spiritual matters, he will become increasingly confused about his world. There *are* reasonable answers to many of life's conflicts and seeming contradictions. One of the finest gifts parents can give a child is a clear understanding of the world and its confusing problems. Without this stable base of knowledge and understanding, is it any wonder many children cry to their parents, "Why didn't you give me a meaning for all this? What's it all about?"

Another reason this wait-and-choose approach to spirituality is grossly negligent is that more and more organizations and cults are offering destructive, enslaving, and false answers to life's questions. These people would like nothing better than to find a person who was brought up in a seemingly broad-minded way. He is easy prey for any group offering concrete answers, no matter how false or enslaving.

It is amazing to me how some parents can spend thousands of dollars and go to any length of political manipulation to make sure their child is well prepared educationally. Yet, for the most important preparation of all, for life's spiritual battles and finding real meaning in life, a child is left to fend for himself and made easy prey to cultists.

Prepare Your Teenagers Spiritually

How do parents prepare their teenagers spiritually? Organized religious instruction and activities are extremely important to a developing child or teenager. However, nothing influences a teenager more than his home and what he is exposed to there. Parents need to be actively involved in a teenager's spiritual growth. They cannot afford to leave it to others, even superb church youth workers.

1. Parents must teach their teenagers spiritual concerns. They must teach them not only spiritual facts, but how to apply them in their everyday life. And this is not easy. It is quite simple to give teenagers basic scriptural facts, such as who different Bible persons were and what they did. But that is not what we are after ultimately. For we want teenagers to understand what meaning biblical characters and principles have for them personally. We can only do this at somewhat of a sacrifice to ourselves, as with focused attention. We must be willing to spend time alone with our teenagers in order to provide for their emotional needs as well as spiritual needs. In fact whenever possible, why not do them simultaneously?

   2. Parents must share their own spiritual experiences. With the factual knowledge gained from church, Sunday School, and home, a teenager only has the raw material with which to grow spiritually. He must learn to use this knowledge effectively and accurately to become a mature person spiritually. To do this a teenager needs the experience of walking with God daily and learning to rely on Him personally.

   The best way to help a teen with this is to share your own spiritual life with him. As a teenager matures, we parents want to gradually increase our sharing with him about how we ourselves love God, walk with Him, rely on Him, seek His guidance and help, thank Him for His love, care, gifts, and answered prayer.

   We want to share these things with our teenager as they happen, not afterward. Only in this way can a teen get "on-the-job" training. Sharing past experiences is simply giving additional factual information, not letting a teenager learn for himself through his own experience. There is a lot of truth in the old statement, "Experience is the best teacher." Let him share in yours. The more a teenager learns to trust God, the stronger he will become.

   Your teenager needs to learn how God meets all personal and family needs, including financial. He needs to know what his parents are praying for. For example, he needs to know when you are praying for the needs of others. When appropriate, he should know of problems for which you are asking God's help. Don't forget to keep him informed about how God is working in your life, and how He is using you to minister to someone. And, of course, your teenager should certainly know you are praying for him and for his particular needs.

   3. Parents should be examples of forgiveness. A teenager must be taught by example how to forgive and how to find forgiveness, both from God and people. Parents do this first of all by forgiving. Next, when they make a mistake which hurts a teenager, they admit the mistake, apologize, and ask his forgiveness. I cannot overstress how important this is. So many people today have problems with guilt. They cannot forgive and/or they cannot feel forgiven. What can be more miserable? But the fortunate person who has learned how to forgive those who offend him, and who is able to ask and receive forgiveness, demonstrates a mark of mental health.

Balcony People

My pastor, Moncrief Jordan, told me a story about a friend of his. And because it has bearing on how we deal with our teenagers I want to tell it to you. Pastor Jordan's friend said that when he was trying to deal with his own tendencies toward discouragement and despair, he would let his "balcony people" speak to his "cellar voices."

The cellar voices in all of us come from the basements of our lives. Sometimes they are impulses and urges we normally associate with the animal kingdom—rash temper, boiling anger, and vindictive feelings.

But the cellar voices go beyond emotional or physical reactions. They proceed from the dark side of ourselves—a dark side that most folks rarely see. The cellar is where our scenarios of hate, greed, pride, lust, and destruction are formed. And woe to that person who does not recognize the potency of this area!

The cellar voices also come from those around us who, because of low self-esteem, guilt, frustration, or pent-up hostility cut us down, telling us how bad the world is, and how bad we are. If we let them, these cellar voices can lead us to despair and hopelessness.

But fortunately, Pastor Jordan's friend also told him about balcony people. These are the people, living and dead, who have lifted us with their love, faith, hope, and courage.

We all need balcony people who show us that we can live above the petty and discordant levels of life. That we do not have to wallow in negativism and despair. That we do not have to let our inner conflicts create havoc in life. That we can live victoriously. The balcony people speak to us both with their talk and their walk.

Some of the balcony people in Scripture are beautifully summarized for us in Hebrews 11, in a roll call of people who proved that faith is workable, and that life can have meaning and purpose at *any* time of history.

Most of us can learn from our own experiences. But it takes a wise person to learn from the experience of others. It is our privilege to let our balcony people save us from unnecessary mistakes and conflicts, and to lift us up in hope.

Perhaps we should consider writing our own "11th chapter of Hebrews," listing our own balcony people. Do you realize we have more balcony people to draw from than any previous people in history?

From our list, there ought to be a select few balcony people who are living today and with whom we can bare our hearts and souls from time to time. These are people we utterly trust and admire, and to whom we can reveal our dark sides, knowing we will be loved and prayed for. That is part of what the church of Christ is all about.

Our teenagers need balcony people to give them hope. They are hearing more than enough cellar voices. We must be balcony people to our precious youth. But we must work at it—we do not have to be spreaders of gloom and doom. Oh, how very sensitive our teenagers are to pessimism, especially from their parents. We do not have to buy into the despair of our day. Faith in our God and in ourselves—have you read the 11th chapter of Hebrews yet? No? Hurry up!—brings a hope that cannot be destroyed.

God gives us hope. Hope is not wishful thinking. Hope is the *knowledge* that the wonderful promises of God are true. There are thousands of promises God has made to us. Read them for yourselves. Start with Romans 8:28—"And we know that all that happens to us is working for our good if we love God and are fitting into His plans" (TLB).

Or how about Jeremiah 29:11: " 'For I know the plans I have for you,' " says the Lord. 'They are plans for good and not for evil, to give you a future and a hope' " (TLB).

Or consider Isaiah 41:10: "Fear not, for I am with you; be not dismayed for I am your God! I will strengthen you, yes, I will help you; yes, I will uphold you with My vindicating right hand" (MLB).

Or look at Psalm 34:19: "Many are the afflictions of the righteous; but out of them all the Lord delivers him" (MLB).

If you would like to write me through Victor Books, P.O. Box 1825, Wheaton, Illinois 60187, I will send you an extensive list of Scripture references which proclaim hope and assurance.

Christian Hope

There *must* be recovery of hope in our land. Our young people need hope to face an uncertain future. I know the situation does not look good right now. But, as in generations past, if we give our youth what they need to face the future, they will then be prepared and will do well. We must give them confidence, courage, moral strength, and a sense of responsibility. But we cannot give them these priceless assets without hope—the sure *knowledge* that God exists, that He loves us, and that His promises are true.

My pastor told me of a man he visited regularly. This man had many physical ailments, and eventually both of his legs had to be amputated. Pastor Jordan thought that this would surely break his joyful and optimistic view of life. But it didn't. The man would still swing himself with a trapeze device from his bed to a wheel chair and roll himself down to the parlor in the very depressing nursing home where he lived. There he would play the piano and sing until he had many others singing with him. During his last years, he was the channel of hope and joy to many people.

Christian hope is not dependent on what the world does to us. It is dependent on what we do in the world as we live in response to God's great love for us.

Fellow parents, it is hard to be a balcony person in the 1980s. I know this. But I will guarantee you that it really pays off, for it is like giving water to a drought-parched earth. And best of all, we are giving our teenagers what they need to become balcony people.

By nature, I am not as much a balcony person as my wife, Pat, is. And it is pure joy to see my daughter follow in her mother's footsteps. She is a balcony person also. How I admire that and try to become more that way!

Let's grow together, fellow parents. By working at it every day, we will gradually become more and more like Christ—the ultimate balcony Person.

12

The Older Adolescent

Train your teenager to cope with real life.

As adolescents near the time of normal separation from home, they still need their parents to help them make that precarious crossing into adulthood. Contrary to what many parents assume, this crossing does not happen instantaneously through a high school graduation or a move out of the house.

The transition into adulthood should be a gradual weaning process for which both parents and teenager prepare.

You first prepare for this change by making sure your teenager has learned to lead an independent life. There may have been "practice runs" at living away from home for periods of time, as your child was growing up, such as summer camp experiences and visits with relatives. Now you need to increase your teenager's self-sufficiency by making sure he can actually take care of himself. Can he do his own laundry? Cook balanced meals for himself? Handle all the other necessities for independent living? These needs are usually overlooked, especially with boys. I have known many instances of a boy living away from home for the first time fixing the same unhealthy, starchy meal over and over, to the point of developing vitamin deficiencies and becoming susceptible to illness.

By the time your adolescent becomes independent, he should be able to handle his own finances. This means budgeting his income and balancing his checkbook. Such items may seem like common sense, trivial matters, but many adults still cannot balance a checkbook, much less discipline themselves to save money.

It takes time to train your teenager to manage his affairs; it never just happens. I am amazed, for example, at how many college students cannot even get up in the morning to arrive in class on time. Self-discipline is best learned before leaving home. Seldom is it sufficiently learned later.

Lifelong habits are usually shaped during later adolescence. Although most of the teenager's adult traits or characteristics have been partly formed, they are usually still changeable. Both parent and teenager should make use of this time to enhance favorable characteristics and hopefully modify less desirable ones.

Goal-Orientation

One of the most important aspects of a teenager's personality is his degree of goal-orientation. No one, and especially a teenager, is perfectly balanced in this area of being goal-oriented. Some people are too goal-oriented, putting almost all their personal resources into reaching what they want—good grades, a college degree, money—to the exclusion of other equally important matters such as fun, relaxation, and personal relationships. A person who is too goal-oriented tends to be perfectionistic, judgmental, rigid in his thinking, opinionated, tense, and worried. He also takes things too seriously and personally. Many people who are reading this book will fit into this category, just as I do.

It is fine to be goal-oriented and conscientious. But people who are excessively so will tend to find life a drudgery with little pleasure. They will also increasingly tend toward depression as they become older, especially during the middle years. They have made reaching for goals their meaning to life. So when they reach those goals, they wonder what meaning is left. If they do not reach their goals, they likewise see little meaning. If your older adolescent has these traits, you can be of tremendous help to him by teaching him to find significance in pleasant hobbies and other means of *relaxation*, and especially to learn the immense value of friends and personal relationships. It is still relatively easy for an older adolescent to change. However, the older a person grows, the more difficult it is to change. The more perfectionist and goal-oriented an adult is, the more apt he is to become dull, depressed, rigid, and unpleasant in his old age.

I am reminded of two people who present stark contrasts in this area. I recently saw a 67-year-old man who had been a hard worker, devoting almost all of his energy to his job. He allowed little time for family, fostered few friendships, and was quite a perfectionist. His life was fairly satisfying until retirement. Without his goal (hard work), he lost most of his meaning in life and rapidly became profoundly depressed. When I saw him, he stared straight ahead, as though he were in a catatonic trance. He could hardly move, and just sat motionless, day after day, until his family brought him for treatment.

The exact opposite is our dear next door neighbor, a widow. She has been a woman of accomplishment, and still is involved in many projects. Yet she has always loved people and fostered close relationships. People feel wonderful just being around her.

What a difference! The man has been too perfectionist and goal-oriented; our neighbor has achieved a wonderful balance. It is important to remember that their personal characteristics were present in late adolescence and simply intensified over the years.

The more a teenager sees the meaning and value of human relationships, the more he will develop into a pleasant, congenial person, who can roll with life's punches without crippling depression The key is *balance*. You want your older adolescent to have the essential degree of goal-orientation to enable him to have a life of satisfying accomplishments. But you also want him to be person-oriented so that he can have truly meaningful personal relationships, as a spouse, parent, and friend.

My precious daughter Carey and I had long discussions along these lines before she went away to college. I emphasized the importance of friendships acquired in high school and college. These are truly special friendships which should be kept alive over the years, if at all possible. I recommended that she keep a notebook with the names and addresses of every meaningful friend she makes, so that she can keep in touch with them over the years.

Although we form close friendships after our school days, there is something special about high school and college friends. These are the people we can call on years later and almost always find an instant rapport. It is as though the conversation simply picks up where it left off—back in the "good old days." Appreciation for friends is especially important for the older adolescent who is so goal-oriented that he tends to devalue friendships.

However, your adolescent may be just the opposite. His orientation may be to relax, have fun, enjoy life, and to delay responsibility as long as possible. As common sense will tell you, these traits should be identified and worked on from very early adolescence.

You may have a teenager who is capable of making good grades, but who is having so much fun in activities and with friends, that he doesn't give proper time and effort to academics. It is appropriate to handle this problem directly, if your child is not strongly passive-aggressive. If you are not dealing with an anger problem, you can help your teenager become more balanced in his approach to responsibility. If you have done your job as a parent, making sure your teenager feels unconditionally loved, you have every right and responsibility to directly enforce your teenager to take the proper amount of responsibility and become properly goal-oriented.

This reminds me of an experience with my 13-year-old David. He is capable of making good grades, and did so until the beginning of the seventh grade when he became so engrossed in football and friends that his report card showed all C's. Knowing this was far below his ability, and seeing his strong drift toward fun and frolic and excessive peer interaction, Pat and I knew we must make some changes. We set up a system calling for each of David's teachers to send home a weekly grade over the six-week grading period. We told David each time a C came home, there would be no sports for the coming week. Guidelines for good study habits were established and enforced. Not only did the next report card reveal all A's, but David's whole attitude toward academics had changed. He really felt good about his success and no longer needed coaxing from us.

Occasionally, an older adolescent will have a negative academic attitude as high school graduation approaches. This often happens to a teen who has had previous learning disabilities or perceptual problems; and it may create conflict with the parents who have high future academic expectations for him. Each situation needs to be considered separately. I have seen many instances of this kind resolved by encouraging the teen to take off a year or two to work or assume military duty. Often this course will give the adolescent the time and experience he needs to mature, settle down, and become appropriately goal-oriented, vocationally and socially.

Preparation for the Real World
One of the most difficult dilemmas that we parents face today is the preparation of our young people to handle the real world with its alcohol and other drugs, sexual license, decaying spiritual values, and general attitude of "meism" or selfishness. This is a difficult subject even to write about, because it is so controversial. I believe it is a cruel blunder to completely isolate children and teenagers from the world as it really is, but I have seen many parents do this. Eventually, of course, they must let their sons or daughters go. If our young people have not learned how to deal with these pressures while living at home, how can they cope with real life when they are on their own?

While your teenager is living at home under its haven of safety and guidance, he needs some exposure to these problem areas, in a controlled way. Of course, I don't mean encouragement or permission to "live it up" for the experience. I mean *training* your teenager how to cope with real life, and setting privileges based on trust, consequences of behavior, and appropriateness of the social occasion. These privileges should be controlled to progress in such a way that you can help your teenager handle different encounters as they arrive. He needs to be well trained on how to handle most of life's situations. Of course, this does not mean that he is to participate in unhealthy activities. Rather, he should learn how to handle himself maturely, and determine to keep himself pure and uncontaminated by the unhealthy aspects of today's society. To achieve such maturity in your teenager will take time, preparation, training, conviction, and self-control on your part.

One of the most serious mistakes you can make is to assume that school, church, or other organizations can or will handle this part of your child's development for you. The parent has the greatest effect on the teenager, especially regarding values and lifestyle. Schools and churches can help, but without the primary involvement of the parent, the teenager will not usually do well. Sending a child off to college without preparation for life is copping out on parental responsibility. I have seen many adolescents who seem to behave well at home go wild as soon as they are away from their parents' control. They haven't learned the self-control necessary to handle independence and freedom.

To help prevent this catastrophe, work with your teenager as he *becomes* independent. You want your teenager to realize that you are working with and not against him, toward his independence and freedom. In doing so, you will want to be careful to follow the guideline of trust vs. consequences. During the few months before the adolescent leaves home, you can gradually make the teenager's privileges similar to those he will have where he is going to live—a college dormitory or apartment. You will be training your teenager to cope by using self-control and taking responsibility, when there is little or no supervision.

Such training is hard on parents. After years of carefully training and supervising our children, we must learn to let our dear ones go, and this is a frightening experience. But it is so much easier and so much more constructive to do it at home in a carefully planned and gradual way, working as a team with our teenagers to accomplish it. This means gradually removing as many rules as possible to give our teenagers a few weeks or months of experience with the independence appropriate for a young adolescent ready to leave home. We have to be careful here. If we have done our job in training our teenagers, they will handle themselves well.

However, there are a few very common conflicts which often arise, and could be disturbing to the rest of the family—such as coming in at late hours and upsetting other family members. Or being inconsiderate in not letting the household know where they will be, especially at mealtimes. Or failing to carry out an expected chore or errand. Or not showing up where and when expected. If such behavior persists, parents need to revert to making privileges contingent on trust and consequences of behavior, since the teen is not ready for full assumption of responsibility.

Security

Although our adolescents are nearing adulthood, their emotional needs have changed little since childhood. Even at this stage, they need to know that we genuinely love them, that we are available, and that we will help them in any way we can, for their own good. As long as they feel we truly care for them, we can continue to have constructive influence in helping them achieve independence.

One problem for many parents at this point is the old enemy—anger. Some parents who handled anger well when their adolescents were younger have a real problem handling it at this critical point. We must remember that this final separation is difficult for our teens. It is a long weaning process during which time we must remain available to offer support and help. Have you ever watched a mother bird push her youngster out of the nest when that time has come? I recently watched several nests of swallows where the mothers were performing this difficult task. Some of the young birds flew with no problems. Some had difficulty learning to fly and mother and father were available to help where needed. Then it happened. One young bird frantically tried to fly but fell through the air. The sickening thud told us the tragedy—it was not ready for departure and the parents were not available to help him in this last phase.

Even after our young person leaves home, *he still needs us*. He needs to know we are there, available, and ready to help when needed. In chapter 9, I mentioned a visit that Pat and I had with Carey's friends at college, during their freshman year. All of these fine young people were happy in school and with their new friends. But they all had the same complaint—they seldom heard from their parents. Not enough calls, letters, or visits.

When we later related this to Carey, she admitted she felt the same way, which surprised me. But after thinking it over and remembering my first days away from home, I began to understand. The weaning from a good parent-child relationship is slow and often painful. Since that weekend, Pat and I have made it a ritual to call Carey every Sunday night to make sure she knows we are here thinking about her, praying for her, and ready to help where we can.

Another characteristic about departing young ones is their need for everything to remain the same—just the way they left it. This helps the young person feel secure. It is a good idea to keep as many things as possible the same—especially rooms and personal possessions. He may feel terribly hurt if his room is turned over to a younger brother or sister. And don't be too quick to sell your house and move to smaller quarters. I've heard several teenagers say, "I sure hope my parents never sell our house. I want always to be able to go back home."

However, the most important anchor of security a teen leaves behind is the marital relationship of his parents. One of the most devastating things that can happen to an adolescent soon after leaving home is the separation or divorce of his parents. It's as though the foundations of his whole world are crumbling. Yet, it is amazing how many parents actually plan to "stay together for the sake of the kids, but as soon as they leave home, we're getting a divorce." This is extraordinarily unwise. Not only is the child's basic foundation crushed, but at the very time when he most needs support—a time when he is desperately trying to adjust to a new life, new friends, etc. In most cases, the young person will be burdened with heavy guilt. Regardless of how unreasonable it may sound, the young person feels that he is somehow responsible, either for the bad marriage or for the divorce. If a divorce is inevitable, it is far better that it take place long enough before the adolescent leaves home, so that he can work through the natural feelings of loss and grief with help of parents, friends, and minister, before he takes on the difficult task of leaving home for the first time.

I know one young man, John, who believed that his parents were happy in their marriage when he left for college. Within three months they were divorced. The mother remarried soon afterward and sold the family house. John seldom goes home because it is so depressing for him. His base of security has been destroyed. You can imagine what this has done to his sense of well-being.

Another important factor as children leave is that they stay involved with sources of security, stability, and growth. One of these is the church. It is important not only to attend church regularly with our children and teenagers, but to do all we can to make the church experience pleasant for them. A good youth group is critical especially in the teen years. As our children move to college or work, we need to encourage them to become involved in church and Christian activities.

Spouse Selection

One of my priorities as a parent is to make sure each of my children can identify the qualities that are desirable in a future spouse. It is not easy for a teenager to identify traits within a peer which indicate the ability to be a good spouse or parent. Because dating is a somewhat artificial situation, a young person often doesn't have much to go on other than how "good" he feels with that person. Of course, simply depending on such superficial feelings can be disastrous. Regularly I counsel young people who have made that tragic mistake. They have depended on their feelings to decide whether to become involved or marry, rather than considering other far more important factors.

One of the first things I taught Carey about this matter was to look at the character of a boy, as well as to consider the feelings he produced in her. I explained to her that the best indicator of how he will treat his wife after marriage is the way he presently treats persons whom he is not required to treat with consideration—those who are elderly, unpleasant, or helpless. I told her to observe how he treated people in service jobs, such as waiters and waitresses.

A third consideration, and the one Carey really latched on to, was to see how he treated and related to children, especially small ones. For you see, Carey has two younger brothers, providing a perfect litmus. Before I gave her these insights, she used to make sure David and Dale were out of sight before a date arrived. After our discussion, Carey would ask David and Dale to answer the door and talk to her date while she "got ready." It was interesting to watch Carey observe her date from a hidden place, to see how he did with her brothers. Our discussion has truly helped Carey gain priceless insight into the boys she has dated.

However, I must admit this did backfire on me once. While at college, she became fond of a student there and brought him home for us to meet. To help him make a good impression on me, she specifically instructed him to treat David and Dale nicely.

Another characteristic of a person who will be a good spouse or parent is his ability to reason. This is critical in marital and parent-child relationships; to be a reasonable person, one must be able to reason. If a person can reason, he usually has the ability to come to an agreement or compromise in family conflicts. In other words, the person can argue from his point of view but is able and willing to be proven wrong or to compromise, and to come to a mutual understanding with spouse or child. On the other hand, a person who cannot reason will almost invariably be unreasonable He will be unable to argue, that is, explain his viewpoint in a conflict, and will probably demand his own way.

These traits, if looked for, can be identified after a short period of time, especially during a situation in which the person is angry. A person who *never* gets angry should be suspect. He could possibly be passive-aggressive, or he may not have the resources to develop a real emotional attachment to anyone. Either of these character types is difficult to live with. However, we must say that there are caring persons who simply are so low-keyed that they seldom are provoked to anger. I envy them. They *are* rare.

Another indicator, which is extremely important but difficult to discern, is a person's ability to manage ambivalence. Ambivalence is having opposite feelings toward the same person. Although ambivalence is difficult to detect, I think the best way to do so is to observe a person's tolerance of different kinds of people. For example, consider the person who has strong and uncompromising opinions about everything. To him, there is no gray area, no room for compromise about anything. He sees people as all right or all wrong, all good or all bad. This person cannot see that there is good and bad, pleasant and unpleasant, in everyone. We all have ambivalent feelings. Handling them well, on a conscious level, is an indicator of maturity. (See chapter 2 of *How to Really Love Your Child* for a deeper discussion of ambivalence.)

Another good way to determine what kind of spouse or parent a person will be is to watch how he gets along with and treats his own parents, brothers, sisters, grandparents, other relatives, and long-time friends. This is an excellent indication of how he will treat his spouse and children in the future.

Be Optimistic

In our discussions about our young people, we have talked about some painful things. But we have also talked about how we *can and should* be optimistic and hopeful about our teenagers and their future. Yes, many of our youth have serious problems—some of them severe. But many are doing beautifully and are a real encouragement to me. Recently we had the college students from our church come to our home for a get-together. What an uplifting time it was for me, with these warm, wholesome, mature, vivacious, and lovable young people. It reaffirmed for me that our efforts are worthwhile.

Dear parent, this book on teenagers was written expressly *for you* by another parent. My strongest desire is to see my children—

and yours—grow into strong, healthy, happy, and independent adults. Some of the material in these chapters may be difficult to fully grasp on the first reading. I strongly suggest that you now reread the book and let the material come together for you in your particular circumstances. We need to be continually reminded how to really love our teenagers.